Closely
Following the
Present Vision
of the Lord's
Recovery

The Holy Word for Morning Revival

Witness Lee

Living Stream Ministry
Anaheim, CA • www.lsm.org

First Edition, December 2007.

ISBN 0-7363-3604-4

Published by

Living Stream Ministry
2431 W. La Palma Ave., Anaheim, CA 92801 U.S.A.
P. O. Box 2121, Anaheim, CA 92814 U.S.A.

Printed in the United States of America

07 08 09 10 11 12 / 9 8 7 6 5 4 3 2 1

Contents

Preface

1. This book is intended as an aid to believers in developing a daily time of morning revival with the Lord in His word. At the same time, it provides a limited review of the Thanksgiving weekend conference held in Boston, Massachusetts, November 22-25, 2007. The subject of the conference was "Closely Following the Present Vision of the Lord's Recovery." Through intimate contact with the Lord in His word, the believers can be constituted with life and truth and thereby equipped to prophesy in the meetings of the church unto the building up of the Body of Christ.

2. The content of this book is taken primarily from the conference message outlines, the text and footnotes of the Recovery Version of the Bible, selections from the writings of Witness Lee and Watchman Nee, and *Hymns,* all of which are published by Living Stream Ministry.

3. The book is divided into weeks. One conference message is covered per week. Each week presents first the message outline, followed by six daily portions, a hymn, and then some space for writing. The message outline has been divided into days, corresponding to the six daily portions. Each daily portion covers certain points and begins with a section entitled "Morning Nourishment." This section contains selected verses and a short reading that can provide rich spiritual nourishment through intimate fellowship with the Lord. The "Morning Nourishment" is followed by a section entitled "Today's Reading," a longer portion of ministry related to the day's main points. Each day's portion concludes with a short list of references for further reading and some space for the saints to make notes concerning their spiritual inspiration, enlightenment, and enjoyment to serve as a reminder of what they have received of the Lord that day.

4. The space provided at the end of each week is for composing a short prophecy. This prophecy can be composed by considering all of our daily notes, the "harvest" of our

inspirations during the week, and preparing a main point with some sub-points to be spoken in the church meetings for the organic building up of the Body of Christ.

5. Following the last week in this volume, we have provided reading schedules for both the Old and New Testaments in the Recovery Version with footnotes. These schedules are arranged so that one can read through both the Old and New Testaments of the Recovery Version with footnotes in two years.

6. As a practical aid to the saints' feeding on the Word throughout the day, we have provided verse cards at the end of the volume, which correspond to each day's scripture reading. These may be removed and carried along as a source of spiritual enlightenment and nourishment in the saints' daily lives.

7. The conference message outlines were compiled by Living Stream Ministry from the writings of Witness Lee and Watchman Nee. The outlines, footnotes, and references in the Recovery Version of the Bible are by Witness Lee. All of the other references cited in this publication are from the published ministry of Witness Lee and Watchman Nee.

Thanksgiving Weekend
Conference
(November 22-25, 2007)

General Subject:

Closely Following the Present Vision
of the Lord's Recovery

Banners:

To live out and work out the New Jerusalem is
to live out and work out God's complete salvation
according to the intrinsic essence
of the unique New Testament ministry
for the reality of the Body of Christ
and a new revival.

God became man so that man may become God
in life and nature but not in the Godhead
to produce and build up the Body of Christ
for the fulfillment of God's economy
to close this age and
bring Christ back to set up His kingdom.

God's intention is, through the universal woman,
to bring forth the man-child—
the stronger part of God's people—
whom He will use to defeat His enemy
and bring in His kingdom.

We must closely follow
the present vision of the Lord's recovery
by holding to the teaching of the apostles
to remain in the essence of oneness.

Closely Following the Present Vision of the Lord's Recovery according to the Intrinsic Essence of the Unique New Testament Ministry

Scripture Reading: 2 Cor. 3:3, 6, 8; 4:1; 5:18-21; 11:2-3; 1 Tim. 1:3-4, 18; Rev. 22:1-2, 14, 17a

Day 1

I. **The vision that the Lord has given to His recovery is an all-inclusive vision, the ultimate consummation of all the visions—the vision of the New Jerusalem (Prov. 29:18a; Acts 26:18-19; 22:15; Rev. 21:2, 9-11):**

A. The totality of what the Bible reveals to us is the New Jerusalem; the New Jerusalem is the total composition of the entire revelation of the Bible (Gen. 28:10-22; John 1:1, 14, 29, 32, 42, 51; Rev. 21:3, 22).

B. Our living out the New Jerusalem is for us to become the New Jerusalem, and our working out the New Jerusalem is for us to build the New Jerusalem by the flowing Triune God (Jer. 2:13; John 4:14b; 7:37-39; Rev. 22:1-2a).

C. Every local church should be a miniature of the New Jerusalem, and every believer should be "a little New Jerusalem"; whatever is ascribed to the New Jerusalem should be both our corporate and personal experience (21:3, 22-23; 22:1-2, 14, 17a; 3:12; Heb. 11:10).

II. **The New Jerusalem is the embodiment of God's complete salvation with its judicial and organic aspects (Rom. 5:10; Rev. 22:14):**

A. God's full salvation is a composition of God's righteousness as the base and God's life as the consummation (Rom. 1:16-17; 5:10, 17-18, 21; Luke 15:22-23; cf. Jer. 2:13; 13:23; 17:9; 23:5-6; 31:33).

B. The entire New Jerusalem is a matter of life built on the foundation of righteousness (Rev. 21:14, 19-20; 22:1; Psa. 89:14; cf. Gen. 9:8-17).

Day 2 C. As we experience each section of God's organic salvation, we go up level by level until we become beings in the New Jerusalem (Rom. 5:10, 17, 21; 8:10, 6, 11; Rev. 22:1-2; cf. Jer. 18:15; Micah 5:2):

1. We are regenerated by participating in God's life to become God's species, God's children, for God's sonship (John 1:12-13; Rev. 21:7; 22:14b).

2. We are sanctified by participating in God's nature to become as holy as the holy city (1 Thes. 5:23; Eph. 5:26).

3. We are renewed by participating in God's mind to become as new as the New Jerusalem (2 Cor. 4:16; Eph. 4:23).

4. We are transformed by participating in God's being to be constituted with the Triune God as gold, silver (pearl), and precious stones (1 Cor. 3:12a; 2 Cor. 3:18; Rom. 12:2; Rev. 21:18-21).

5. We are conformed to the image of the first-born Son of God by participating in God's image to have the appearance of the New Jerusalem (Rom. 8:28-29; Rev. 21:11; 4:3).

6. We are glorified by participating in God's glory to be completely permeated with the glory of the New Jerusalem (Rom. 8:21; Phil. 3:21; Rev. 21:11).

Day 3 III. **To live out and work out the New Jerusalem is to live out and work out God's complete salvation according to the intrinsic essence of the unique New Testament ministry for the reality of the Body of Christ and a new revival (Phil. 1:19; 2:13; Rom. 5:10, 17; 2 Cor. 3:18; 4:1, 16; Eph. 4:11-12, 16):**

A. The ministry of the Spirit is the ministry of the new covenant to deify us by inscribing our hearts with the Spirit of the living God as the divine and mystical "ink," making us the living letters of Christ—this is the highest peak of the divine revelation (2 Cor. 3:3, 6, 8, 18; 4:1; Isa. 42:6; 49:6; Psa. 45:1-2):

1. By the ministry of the Spirit, we are "Christ-ified" to become the city of life and the bride of Christ; thus, the Spirit as the consummated Triune God marries the bride as the transformed tripartite church to live a life that is the mingling of God and man as one spirit, a life that is super-excellent and that overflows with blessings and joy (Rom. 5:10; Rev. 2:7; 22:1-2, 17a).

2. In order to be constituted as the ministers of the new covenant for the building up of the Body of Christ, we must experience all the aspects of the all-inclusive Spirit in 2 Corinthians—the anointing Spirit, the sealing Spirit, the pledging Spirit (1:21-22; 5:5), the inscribing Spirit (3:3), the life-giving Spirit (v. 6), the ministering Spirit (v. 8), the freeing Spirit (v. 17), the transforming Spirit (v. 18), and the transmitting Spirit (13:14).

B. The ministry of righteousness is the ministry of Christ as our objective righteousness for our justification and as our subjective righteousness "embroidered" into us by the transforming work of the Spirit for the living out and genuine expression of Christ—this is the God-man living (3:9; Psa. 45:13-14; Rom. 8:4; Psa. 23:3):

Day 4

1. By the ministry of righteousness, we receive Christ as our objective righteousness and we enjoy Him as our subjective righteousness in order that we may become the New Jerusalem as the new creation of righteousness in the new heaven and new earth (1 Cor. 1:30; Phil. 3:9; 2 Pet. 3:13; cf. Isa. 33:22).

2. Objective righteousness (Christ given to us) issues in grace (Christ enjoyed by us), and grace issues in subjective righteousness (Christ lived out of us) (Rom. 5:1-2, 17-18; Luke 15:22-23).

3. The power of grace operates in us and produces subjective righteousness, making us right with God, with others, and even with ourselves; it not only subdues sin but also overcomes Satan and death in our being, causing us to reign in life (2 Tim. 2:1; Rom. 5:17, 21).

4. The righteousness that we receive for our justification is objective and enables us to meet the requirements of the righteous God, whereas the righteousnesses of the overcoming saints are subjective and enable them to meet the requirements of the overcoming Christ (Rev. 22:14; 19:7-8).

Day 5 C. The ministry of reconciliation is the ministry of reconciling the world to Christ through the forgiveness of sins for their judicial redemption and of reconciling the believers to Christ that they might be persons who live in the spirit, in the Holy of Holies, for their organic salvation— this is shepherding people according to God (2 Cor. 5:18-21; 1 Pet. 5:1-6; Heb. 13:20):

1. The Lord's present recovery is to bring us into the reality of Christ's pneumatic shepherding in Psalm 23 as the issue of His redeeming death and church-producing resurrection in Psalm 22 and as the accomplishing factor of His coming as the King to establish His kingdom in Psalm 24.

2. By the ministry of reconciliation we are shepherded into God to enjoy Him as the springs of waters of life so that we may become the eternal Zion as the corporate Holy of Holies, the place where God is (Rev. 7:14, 17; 14:1;

21:16, 22; Psa. 20:2; 24:1, 3, 7-10; 48:2; 50:2; 87:2; 125:1; Ezek. 48:35b).

3. The ministry of reconciliation is the apostolic ministry in cooperation with Christ's heavenly ministry to shepherd the flock of God for building up the Body of Christ to consummate the New Jerusalem according to God's eternal economy (John 21:15-17; Acts 20:28-29; Rev. 1:12-13).

Day 6 IV. **The Lord's recovery brings us back to the unique ministry of the New Testament; this ministry (2 Cor. 4:1) has the following characteristics:**

A. It ministers the healthy teaching of God's economy and wars the good warfare against the different and strange teachings of the dissenters with the strange fire of man's natural enthusiasm, natural affection, natural strength, and natural ability (1 Tim. 1:3-4, 18; Heb. 13:9; 2 Tim. 2:1-15; Lev. 10:1-11).

B. It produces the local churches as the golden lampstands to be the testimony of Jesus with the same essence, appearance, and expression (Rev. 1:10-13, 20).

C. It builds up the one Body of Christ by the one Spirit, perfecting all of us into the oneness of the Triune God (John 17:23; Eph. 4:1-4, 11-13; Zech. 4:6).

D. It prepares the overcomers to be Christ's bride, His "queen," in Himself as the "royal abode" and in the local churches as the "palaces of ivory" to consummate in the New Jerusalem as the "King's palace" (Psa. 45:1-15; Rev. 21:2, 9-10).

E. It betroths us to Christ, stirring up our love for Him in the simplicity and the purity toward Christ to make us His queen (2 Cor. 11:2-3; Psa. 45:9-15).

F. It strengthens us to follow Christ in the fellowship of His sufferings on the pathway to glory,

the way of the cross, for the manifestation and
multiplication of life (John 12:24-26; Col. 1:24;
2 Cor. 4:10-11, 16-18; 11:23-33).

G. It dispenses Christ as grace, truth, life, and the
Spirit into us for our revelation of Christ, our
enjoyment of Christ, and our growth in life so
that we may be saved in life to reign in life (1:10,
24; Phil. 1:25; Rom. 5:10, 17).

H. It sanctifies us through the word of the truth
and through the washing of the water in the
word (John 17:17; Eph. 5:26).

I. It shepherds us with the cherishing and nour-
ishing presence of the pneumatic Christ (vv. 29-
30; Rev. 1:12-13).

J. It tears down hierarchy and blends us into
one, making us all brothers of Christ, slaves of
Christ, and members of Christ to be the one
Body of Christ in reality (Matt. 23:8-12; Phil.
2:1-4; 1 Cor. 12:24; cf. 3 John 9).

K. It tears down the high places and exalts Christ
alone to make Christ everything in the church
(Deut. 12:1-3; 2 Cor. 4:5; 10:3-5; Col. 3:10-11).

L. It brings all of us into function to practice the
God-ordained way (Rom. 12:4-5; 1 Cor. 14:4b, 31;
Eph. 4:11-12).

M. It leads us to follow the Lamb wherever He may
go for the preaching of the gospel of the kingdom to the whole inhabited earth (Rev. 14:4;
Matt. 24:14).

N. It brings us into a new revival of living out the
New Jerusalem and working out the New Jerusalem to gain the reality of the Body of Christ
as the highest peak in God's economy (2 Cor. 3:6,
8-9; 5:18-20; Rom. 12:4-5; Eph. 4:4-6, 16).

Morning Nourishment

Rev. And I saw the holy city, New Jerusalem, coming
21:2 down out of heaven from God, prepared as a bride
adorned for her husband.

22:1-2 And he showed me a river of water of life, bright as
crystal, proceeding out of the throne of God and of
the Lamb in the middle of its street. And on this
side and on that side of the river was the tree of
life, producing twelve fruits, yielding its fruit each
month; and the leaves of the tree are for the healing of the nations.

The sixty-six books of the entire Bible reveal many things to
us. When all these things are embodied together as one entity,
that is the New Jerusalem. The sixty-six books of the Bible consummate in the New Jerusalem. The totality of all the positive
things recorded in the sixty-six books of the Bible is the New
Jerusalem. On the one hand, we may say that the Bible unveils
to us the central line of the divine revelation, which is God's
economy and God's dispensing. On the other hand, we may say
in brief that the totality of what the Bible reveals to us is the
New Jerusalem. The New Jerusalem is the total composition of
the entire revelation of the Bible.

The foundation of the New Jerusalem consists of twelve
layers of precious stones (Rev. 21:14, 19-20),...and the colors of
the twelve layers of precious stones in the foundation of the New
Jerusalem look like a rainbow. According to Genesis 9:8-17, the
rainbow is a sign that reminds us of God's faithfulness in keeping His word. God's faithfulness is based on His righteousness. If
there were no righteousness, there would be no faithfulness.
Thus, the foundation of the New Jerusalem is the righteousness
of God with God's faithfulness. (*Life-study of Isaiah,* p. 348)

Today's Reading

Within the New Jerusalem there is a river of life, which flows,
or spirals, from the top of the city to the bottom, to reach all the

twelve gates (Rev. 22:1). That flowing of the river of life saturates the entire city. On the two sides of the river the tree of life grows. Thus, the content of the New Jerusalem is life. Within the city the river of life flows and the tree of life grows as a vine along the two banks of the river, to supply the entire city. This indicates that the entire New Jerusalem is a matter of life built on the foundation of righteousness. Life is the consummation of righteousness, and righteousness is the base, the foundation, of life.

The New Jerusalem is the embodiment of God's full salvation, and God's full salvation is a composition of God's righteousness as the base and God's life as the consummation. This is the revelation of the Bible. (*Life-study of Isaiah*, pp. 348-349)

When we get into the full record concerning the New Jerusalem, we will spontaneously understand that this is fully related to our personal experiences of the Triune God. Do not think that the New Jerusalem is merely something objective in the future for a certain group of people. We have to realize that what is recorded in Revelation 21 and 22 should be experienced by us today in a very personal way. Experientially speaking, every proper and normal Christian is "a little New Jerusalem." Whatever is ascribed to the New Jerusalem corporately should be experienced by us individually and personally. With and in each one of us are the three gates of the Divine Trinity. Furthermore, in each one of us there must be the throne of God and of the Lamb. We must enthrone Him in our heart and in our spirit. In other words, in the very center of our being there should be the throne of God and of the Lamb. At the end of the record of the New Jerusalem the unique item is the throne. (*God's New Testament Economy*, pp. 387-388)

Further Reading: The Vision of the Age, chs. 1-3; Words of Training for the New Way, vol. 1, ch. 2; The Practical Points concerning Blending, ch. 5; Life-study of Isaiah, msgs. 46-47; God's New Testament Economy, ch. 38; Crystallization-study of the Gospel of John, msgs. 13-14, 16

Enlightenment and inspiration: _____

_____

_____

_____

Morning Nourishment

**2 Pet. Through which He has granted to us precious and
1:4 exceedingly great promises that through these you
might become partakers of the divine nature, having
escaped the corruption which is in the world by lust.**

As God-men we have the divine right to participate in God's divinity. The phrase *participate in* means…that we possess something and that we enjoy what we possess. We, the God-men, have the divine right to participate…in God's divinity, that is, participate in God.

We human beings were created by God for this purpose. Man was created in God's image and after His likeness (Gen. 1:26)….However, at the time of creation, man did not have God's life. But now as God-men, those who have been born of God to be children of God, we have the right to participate in what God is and even to become God in life, in nature, and in expression but not in the Godhead.

First, as the God-men we have the divine right to participate in God's life. John 3:15 tells us that everyone who believes in the Lord Jesus will have eternal life. Eternal life is the divine life, the life of God. We are human beings, but we can have God's life. We were created in God's image and God's likeness but without God's life. Through regeneration we have been graced by God with His divine life. Through regeneration He has put, has dispensed, His life into our being. (*Incarnation, Inclusion, and Intensification,* pp. 40-41)

Today's Reading

As God-men we also have the divine right to participate in God's nature. Ephesians 1:4 says, "He chose us in Him before the foundation of the world to be holy."…*Holy* means not only sanctified, separated unto God, but also different, distinct, from everything common. God is holy, but we are common….Holiness is His nature. God intends to make us holy even as He is holy (1 Pet. 1:15-16). To be holy is to participate in God's holy nature….God makes us holy by imparting Himself, the Holy One, into our being, so that our whole being may be saturated and permeated with His holy nature….To be holy is to partake of God's divine nature (2 Pet. 1:4). Thus, we may participate not only in God's life but also in God's nature.

Because we have become God-men through regeneration, we also have the right to participate in God's mind....Philippians 2:5 says, "Let this mind be in you, which was also in Christ Jesus."...Ephesians 4:23 says, "Be renewed in the spirit of your mind." The spirit here is the regenerated spirit of the believers, which is mingled with the indwelling Spirit of God. Such a mingled spirit spreads into our mind, thus becoming the spirit of our mind....This is to make His mind our mind, and this is to participate in God's mind.

Next, the God-men have the divine right to participate in God's being....[We are] being transformed into the Lord's image "even as from the Lord Spirit" [2 Cor. 3:18]. This indicates that the work of transformation is done not by something of the Lord Spirit but by the Lord Spirit Himself. Hence, we are being transformed with God's very being.

As God-men we also have the divine right to participate in God's image....We are being "transformed into the same image" [2 Cor. 3:18]....In God's creation man was made in God's image in an outward way, but the image into which we are being transformed is something inward. To be transformed into the same image is to be conformed to the resurrected and glorified Christ as the firstborn Son of God, to be made the same as He is (Rom. 8:29).

Eventually, we will be brought into God's glory to participate in His glory. Hebrews 2:10 says that God is leading many sons into glory. Paul refers to this in Romans 8:30: "...Those whom He justified, these He also glorified." Glorification is the step in God's complete salvation in which God will completely saturate our body with the glory of His life and nature. In this way He will transfigure our body, conforming it to the resurrected, glorious body of His Son (Phil. 3:21). This is the ultimate step in God's organic salvation, wherein God obtains a full expression, which will be manifested ultimately in the New Jerusalem. (*Incarnation, Inclusion, and Intensification,* pp. 41-43)

Further Reading: Incarnation, Inclusion, and Intensification, ch. 4; The God-men, ch. 4

Enlightenment and inspiration: _____

_____
_____
_____

Morning Nourishment

2 Cor. Since you are being manifested that you are a letter
3:3 of Christ ministered by us, inscribed not with ink
but with the Spirit of the living God; not in tablets of
stone but in tablets of hearts of flesh.
6 Who has also made us sufficient as ministers of a
new covenant, *ministers* not of the letter but of the
Spirit; for the letter kills, but the Spirit gives life.
9 For if there is glory with the ministry of condemnation, much more the ministry of righteousness
abounds with glory.

In 2 Corinthians 3:3 the word "ministered" actually means
served. The Greek word means to serve something to someone,
for example, as a waiter serves in a restaurant or a stewardess on
an airplane. Thus, Paul is saying that the Corinthian believers
are a letter of Christ served by the apostles. However, realizing
that the word serve is not adequate, Paul went on to use the word
"inscribed." This explains the meaning of ministered, served.
Paul's way of ministering was by inscribing.

In 3:3 Paul says "inscribed not *with* ink"; he does not say
"inscribed not *by* ink." The word "with" indicates that the spiritual
ink, the Spirit of the living God, is an essence, an element, used by
the one doing the inscribing or the writing. It is important that we
pay careful attention to Paul's use of the preposition "with." This
preposition indicates that the Spirit is neither the writer nor the
instrument used for writing; rather, the Spirit is the essence, the
element, the substance, used in writing. The Spirit of the living
God, who is the living God Himself, is not an instrument, such as
a pen, but an element, the heavenly ink used in writing, with
which the apostles minister Christ as the content for the writing
of living letters that convey Christ. (*Life-study of 2 Corinthians,*
pp. 215-216)

Today's Reading

The ministry of the new covenant is not that of mere teaching.
None of your teachers in school ever inscribed an essence into

your being. They may have put concepts into you, but they did not deposit the essence of anything into you. However, the new covenant ministry does more than merely teach us; it inscribes us. Furthermore, this new covenant ministry inscribes us not with concepts, knowledge, or theology, but with an essence, with something real and substantial....Through the new covenant ministry Christ has been inscribed into us. A divine essence has been written into our being, and this essence is the Spirit.

[In 2 Corinthians 3:9] the phrase "the ministry of condemnation" also refers to the Mosaic ministry of the old covenant....As the old covenant ministry was of death and condemnation, so the new covenant ministry is of the Spirit and of righteousness. Death is versus life, which is embodied in the Spirit, and condemnation is versus righteousness.

Based upon the principle that the Spirit in this chapter is an essence, righteousness here should also be regarded as an essence. Hence, the new covenant ministry has an essence in two aspects: the first aspect is of the Spirit, and the second aspect is of righteousness.

The new covenant ministry...has a substance, and it also has an appearance, an expression. The substance of the new covenant ministry is the Spirit, and the expression, the appearance, is righteousness.

Anyone who has been inscribed with the Spirit of the living God will have an expression of righteousness in his daily living....If you experience the Spirit inwardly and express righteousness outwardly, others will realize that something is different about you. This is the result of the new covenant ministry. This ministry inscribes an essence into our being, an essence that has an inner aspect and an outer aspect. The inner aspect is the living Spirit moving in us; the outer aspect is righteousness as our expression. (*Life-study of 2 Corinthians,* pp. 217, 219-221)

Further Reading: Life-study of 2 Corinthians, msgs. 25-28; *The Experience of Christ as Life for the Building Up of the Church,* chs. 8-9

Enlightenment and inspiration: _____

_____

_____

_____

Morning Nourishment

Rom. For if, by the offense of the one, death reigned through
5:17 the one, much more those who receive the abundance
of grace and of the gift of righteousness will reign in
life through the One, Jesus Christ.

There are two aspects of Christ being righteousness from God
to the believers. The first aspect is that He is the believers' righteousness for them to be justified before God objectively at the
time of their repenting unto God and believing into Christ (Rom.
3:24-26; Acts 13:39; Gal. 3:24b, 27). The first stanza of *Hymns,* #295
says, "God's Christ, who is my righteousness, / My beauty is, my
glorious dress." Christ is our beauty given by God to us to be put on
us as our clothing, our glorious dress. This is outward, objective.

The second aspect is that Christ is the believers' righteousness
lived out of them as the manifestation of God, who is the righteousness in Christ given to the believers for them to be justified by
God subjectively (Rom. 4:25; 1 Pet. 2:24a; James 2:24; Matt. 5:20;
Rev. 19:8). We...repented to God and believed into the Lord Jesus.
Right away God gave Christ to us as a glorious dress to cover us,
so we are acceptable to God righteously, outwardly. This is objective righteousness. Also, when Christ was given to us to be put
on us, He entered into us to be our life and life supply to live Himself out of us. This living out is the manifestation of God in Christ.
This is pleasant in the eyes of God. Surely, God would justify
us subjectively, not just objectively. Now we can see the two
aspects—outward and inward. Christ is put on us, and Christ
enters into us to live God out of us to be our subjective righteousness. (*Crystallization-study of the Epistle to the Romans,* pp. 53-54)

Today's Reading

These two aspects are typified by the best robe and the fattened
calf in Luke 15:22-23. The best robe typifies Christ as God's righteousness given to the believers to cover them outwardly before God
as their objective righteousness. The fattened calf typifies Christ as
God's righteousness given to the believers as their life supply for
them to live out God in Christ as their subjective righteousness.

These two aspects of Christ as righteousness are also typified by the two garments of the queen in Psalm 45:13-14. Solomon had a queen, and that queen had two garments. The first one corresponds with the objective righteousness, which is for our justification. The other garment corresponds with the subjective righteousnesses (Rev. 19:8), which are for our victory. This garment is equivalent to the wedding garment in Matthew 22:11-12.

Romans 5:17 tells us that death reigns through Adam. But we need to be those who receive the abundance of two things: the abundance of grace and the abundance of the gift of righteousness....Here the righteousness is objective. The objective righteousness has been given to us as a gift. Also, Romans 3:24 says that we are justified freely by His grace....We believers have received two things in abundance: the abundance of grace and the abundance of the gift of righteousness.

"The gift of righteousness erases judgment. Judgment comes from sin, but righteousness comes from grace. Righteousness always accompanies grace and is its result. Subjective righteousness (4:25b) comes from grace (vv. 17, 19), and grace comes from objective righteousness (vv. 1-2)" [Rom. 5:17, footnote 2].

Objective righteousness is Christ as God's righteousness given to us to be our righteousness, and this righteousness erases God's righteous judgment on us, the sinners. Adam brought judgment to us through sin. Christ as righteousness erases this judgment. Judgment comes from sin, but righteousness comes from grace. Grace is also Christ. It is God in the Son to be enjoyed by us. Objective righteousness issues in grace, and grace issues in subjective righteousness. Eventually, all three—objective righteousness, grace, and subjective righteousness—are Christ Himself. Objective righteousness is Christ given to us, grace is Christ enjoyed by us, and subjective righteousness is Christ lived out of us. (*Crystallization-study of the Epistle to the Romans*, pp. 54-55, 60-61)

Further Reading: Crystallization-study of the Epistle to the Romans, msgs. 5-6; *Life-study of 2 Corinthians,* msg. 29

Enlightenment and inspiration: _____
_____
_____
_____

Morning Nourishment

2 Cor. But all things are out from God, who has reconciled
5:18-20 us to Himself through Christ and has given to us the
ministry of reconciliation; namely, that God in Christ
was reconciling the world to Himself, not accounting
their offenses to them, and has put in us the word of
reconciliation. On behalf of Christ then we are ambassadors, as God entreats *you* through us; we beseech
you on behalf of Christ, Be reconciled to God.

Paul's word in verse 20 about being reconciled to God is not
directed to sinners; it is directed to the believers in Corinth. These
believers had already been reconciled to God partially....In 1 Corinthians 1 Paul refers to them as saints, as those who had been called
by God into the fellowship of His Son. Therefore, they surely had
been reconciled to God to some degree.

The books of 1 and 2 Corinthians show that the believers at Corinth, after being reconciled to God partially, still lived in the flesh, in
the outward man. Between them and God there was the separat-
ing veil of the flesh, of the natural man. This veil corresponds to the
veil inside the tabernacle, the veil that separated the Holy Place
from the Holy of Holies, not to the veil at the entrance to the Holy
Place. The Corinthian believers may have been in the Holy Place,
but they were not in the Holy of Holies....They were still separated
from the place where God is. Therefore, they had not been reconciled to God in full. (*Life-study of 2 Corinthians*, pp. 322-323)

Today's Reading

In 2 Corinthians 5:19 it is the world that is to be reconciled to
God. In verse 20 it is the believers, those who have already been
reconciled to God, who are to be reconciled to Him further. This
clearly indicates that there are two steps for people to be fully reconciled to God. The first step is as sinners to be reconciled to God
from sin. For this purpose Christ died for our sins (1 Cor. 15:3)
that they may be forgiven by God. This is the objective aspect of
Christ's death. In this aspect He bore our sins on the cross that
God might judge them upon Him for us. The second step is as

believers living in the natural life to be reconciled to God from the flesh. For this purpose Christ died for us—the persons—that we may live to Him in resurrection life (2 Cor. 5:14-15). This is the subjective aspect of Christ's death. In this aspect, for us He was made sin to be judged and done away with by God that we may become the righteousness of God in Him. By the two aspects of His death He has fully reconciled God's chosen people to God.

These two steps of reconciliation are clearly portrayed by the two veils of the tabernacle. The first veil is called a screen (Exo. 26:36). A sinner was brought to God through the reconciliation of the atoning blood to enter into the Holy Place by passing this screen. This typifies the first step of reconciliation. The second veil (Exo. 26:31-35; Heb. 9:3) still separated him from God who is in the Holy of Holies. This veil needed to be rent that he might be brought to God in the Holy of Holies. This is the second step of reconciliation. The Corinthian believers had been reconciled to God, for they had passed through the first veil and had entered into the Holy Place. But they still lived in the flesh. They needed to pass the second veil, which has already been rent (Matt. 27:51; Heb. 10:20), to enter into the Holy of Holies to live with God in their spirit (1 Cor. 6:17). The goal of this Epistle is to bring them here that they may be persons in the spirit (1 Cor. 2:14), in the Holy of Holies. This is what the apostle means by saying, "Be reconciled to God."

The blessings of God can be found in the Holy Place, but God Himself is in the Holy of Holies. In the Holy Place are the blessings of the Spirit...but...not the direct presence of God. In order to have God Himself, we must be reconciled further and come into the Holy of Holies. We must take the second step of reconciliation to be brought into the presence of God. This is full reconciliation. This reconciliation brings us not only out of sin, but also out of the flesh, the natural man, the natural being. Then we are brought to God and become one with Him. (*Life-study of 2 Corinthians,* pp. 323-325)

Further Reading: Life-study of 2 Corinthians, msg. 37; *Life-study of the Psalms,* msg. 11

Enlightenment and inspiration: _____

_____

_____

_____

Morning Nourishment

2 Cor. **Therefore having this ministry as we have been**
4:1 **shown mercy, we do not lose heart.**

11:2-3 **For I am jealous over you with a jealousy of God; for I betrothed you to one husband to present *you as* a pure virgin to Christ. But I fear lest somehow, as the serpent deceived Eve by his craftiness, your thoughts would be corrupted from the simplicity and the purity toward Christ.**

Paul's word in 2 Corinthians 11:2...touches our heart in a deep way and stirs up our love for the Lord Jesus. Very often the Life-study messages touch our hearts in the same way. After reading a few pages of a message, the tender feeling within you for the Lord Jesus is stirred up, and you realize afresh how dear and precious He is....The [opposers] stir up questions, but the genuine ministry stirs up our love for the Lord Jesus as our Bridegroom.

Today's Judaizers seek to shake the believers away from simply loving the Lord Jesus....In chapter eleven Paul has some strong things to say concerning the Judaizers, the false apostles. But before he utters such words, he reminds the believers at Corinth that he has engaged them to one Husband, not to present them as students of theology, but to present them as a pure virgin to Christ.

Whenever there is the preaching of the genuine gospel and the real Jesus with a sincere spirit, the Lord Jesus will be ministered to others so that they may appreciate Him, love Him, follow Him, and take Him as everything. Throughout the centuries, many have preached from the Bible and taught the Bible, but their preaching and teaching nevertheless distracted the believers from the precious person of the Lord Jesus Christ. In principle, such ones distract the believers in the same way as that taken by the serpent in Genesis 3. (*Life-study of 2 Corinthians*, pp. 462-463, 467-468)

Today's Reading

Psalm 45:8b says, "From palaces of ivory, harpstrings have made You glad." In this verse palaces signify local churches; ivory signifies the resurrection life of Christ (John 19:36); and

harpstrings signify praises. The local churches, which are beautiful in the eyes of the Lord and which are His expression, are built
with the resurrection life of Christ, and from the local churches
are the praises that make Him glad. As we praise the Lord, we
need to appreciate what He is in His virtues and what He has
done to produce the church to be His expression. In a very real
sense, Christ's garments, His virtues, have produced the church
as His expression, and both His garments and the church are full
of sweetness.

[In Psalm 45] the king typifies Christ,...the queen typifies the
church, and...those around the queen typify the believers. In
type, this queen is...corporate. The believers are the constituents,
the components, of this corporate queen. Actually, the believers
are both the constituents of the queen and the honorable and
beautiful women.

The situation is the same in Revelation 19:7 and 9a. Verse 7
says, "Let us rejoice and exult, and let us give the glory to Him, for
the marriage of the Lamb has come, and His wife has made herself ready." This verse speaks of the wife of the Lamb. However,
verse 9a says, "Blessed are they who are called to the marriage
dinner of the Lamb." This verse speaks of those who are invited to
the Lamb's marriage dinner....The wife, the bride of Christ, here
is not the church but the overcomers....The guests also are the
overcomers....On the one hand, the overcomers are the bride, and
...on the other hand, they are the guests....In Psalm 45 the bride
of Christ is typified by the queen, and His overcoming guests are
typified by the honorable women around the queen. The bride of
Christ, therefore, is actually the group of overcomers. (*Life-study
of the Psalms,* pp. 256, 260)

Further Reading: Truth Messages, ch. 4; *Elders' Training, Book 1: The
Ministry of the New Testament,* ch. 1; *Elders' Training, Book 3:
The Way to Carry Out the Vision,* ch. 4; *Remaining in the Unique
New Testament Ministry of God's Economy under the Proper
Leadership in His Move; Life-study of the Psalms,* msgs. 20-21

Enlightenment and inspiration: _____

_____

_____

_____

Hymns, #170

1   Lord, Thou art the lovely Bridegroom,
       God appointed, dear to us;
     Thy dear self is so attractive,
       To our heart so beauteous!

2   Dear Beloved, we admire Thee,
       Who can tell Thy preciousness;
     All Thy love we deeply treasure
       And Thine untold loveliness.

3   Thou art fairer than the fairest,
       Thou art sweeter than the sweet;
     Thou art meek and Thou art gracious,
       None can e'er with Thee compete.

4   Full of myrrh are all Thy garments,
       And Thy lips are filled with grace;
     In the savor of Thy suffering,
       We in love Thyself embrace.

5   It is with the oil of gladness
       Thy God hath anointed Thee;
     From the palaces of ivory
       Praise shall ever rise to Thee.

6   God hath blessed Thee, Lord, forever,
       Thou hast won the victory;
     Now we see Thee throned in glory
       With Thy pow'r and majesty.

7   Thou art the desire of nations,
       All Thy worth they'll ever prove;
     Thou, the chiefest of ten thousand,
       Ever worthy of our love.

Composition for prophecy with main point and sub-points: _____
_____
_____
_____
_____
_____
_____
_____
_____
_____
_____
_____
_____
_____
_____
_____
_____
_____
_____
_____
_____
_____
_____
_____
_____
_____
_____
_____
_____
_____
_____
_____
_____
_____
_____
_____
_____
_____

**The High Peak of the Divine Revelation
and the Reality of the Body of Christ**

Scripture Reading: Rom. 8:3; 1:3-4; 8:4; 12:4-5; Gal. 2:20;
Phil. 3:10-11

Day 1 I. **The high peak of the divine revelation is that God became man so that man may become God in life and nature but not in the Godhead to produce and build up the organic Body of Christ for the fulfillment of God's economy to close this age and bring Christ back to set up His kingdom (John 1:12-14; 1 John 3:1-2; Rom. 8:3; 12:4-5; Rev. 11:15):**

A. God's economy is His intention to dispense Himself in His Divine Trinity into His chosen and redeemed people to be their life and nature so that they may be the same as He is for His corporate expression (1 Tim. 1:4; Eph. 1:3-23).

B. God has a heart's desire and eternal purpose; He wants to make Himself man and to make man God so that the two—God and man—may be the same in life and nature (vv. 5, 9; 3:11; 4:16; 5:30, 32).

C. For the accomplishment of His economy, God created us in His own image with the intention that we would become God in life and nature but not in the Godhead (Gen. 1:26; Rev. 4:3; 21:10-11).

Day 2 D. God's economy, as recorded in the Scriptures, is that God became man to make us God in life, nature, and expression so that we may have a God-man living and become the Body of Christ (Rom. 8:3; 1:3-4; 8:4, 14, 29; 12:4-5):

1. God sent His Son to be a man and to live a God-man life by the divine life (John 3:16; 1:14; 6:57a).

2. This God-man living issues in a universal, great man who is exactly the same as Christ—a corporate God-man who lives a God-man

life by the divine life for the manifestation of
God in the flesh (Eph. 4:24; 1 Tim. 3:15-16).

E. God redeemed us for the purpose of making us
God in life and nature so that God can have the
Body of Christ, which consummates in the New
Jerusalem as God's enlargement and expres-
sion for eternity (Eph. 1:6; 4:16; Rev. 21:2).

F. The One who is God yet man dwells in the one
who is man yet God, and the one who is man yet
God dwells in the One who is God yet man; thus,
they are a mutual dwelling place (John 14:2-3,
20, 23; 15:4a).

Day 3   G. God became man to make man God in life and
nature through a marvelous process:

1. With God this process was incarnation,
human living, crucifixion, and resurrection
(1:14; 6:57a; 1:29; 3:14; 12:24; 20:22).

2. With us this process is regeneration, sanctification, renewing, transformation, conformation, and glorification (3:6; Rom. 12:2).

3. In Paul's Epistles we see the ascended
Christ ministering Himself to us as the
life-giving Spirit to transform us into His
image, making us the same as He is in
His essence, element, nature, and appearance (2 Cor. 3:17-18).

H. It is only by God's becoming man to make man
God that the Body of Christ can be produced
and built up; this is the high peak of the divine
revelation given to us by God (Rom. 8:3; 1:3-4;
8:14, 16, 29; 12:4-5).

Day 4   **II. The reality of the Body of Christ is a corporate living by a group of God's redeemed
who have been made God, the God-men, by
God and who live not by themselves but
by another life, which is the processed and
consummated Triune God (Gal. 2:20):**

A. The highest peak in God's economy is the reality
of the Body of Christ; the reality of the Body of

Christ is absolutely organic (Rom. 8:2, 6, 10-11; 12:4-5).

B. The reality of the Body of Christ is the union and mingling of God and man to live out a corporate God-man (John 14:20; 15:4a; Eph. 4:4-6, 24).

C. The reality of the Body of Christ is a corporate living of conformity to the death of Christ by the power of resurrection (Phil. 3:10).

D. The reality of the Body of Christ requires the believers to be absolutely in the resurrection life of Christ; to be in resurrection means that our natural life is crucified and that the God-created part of our being is uplifted in resurrection to be one with Christ in resurrection (John 11:25; Phil. 3:10-11; 2 Cor. 1:9).

Day 5 E. The Lord's recovery is for the building up of the Body of Christ; thus, to know the Body is the proper recovery of the Lord (1 Cor. 12:27; Eph. 4:16; Col. 3:15):

1. God's economy is to gain a Body for His Son; this Body fulfills God's desire for His expression and the destruction of the enemy (Eph. 1:22-23; 4:16; Gen. 1:26-28).

2. The church takes the Body of Christ as its organic factor; without the Body of Christ, the church is lifeless and is a mere human organization (1 Cor. 1:2; 12:12-13, 27).

3. The Body is the intrinsic significance of the church; without the Body, the church makes no sense and has no meaning (Rom. 12:4-5; 16:1, 4, 16).

4. The Body of Christ is formed by Christ as life in us; this life mingles with us to become the Body of Christ (1 John 5:11-12; Col. 1:18; 2:19; 3:4, 15).

5. The Body of Christ is a matter of the mingled spirit; to be in the reality of the Body of Christ is to live in the mingled spirit (Rom. 8:4; 1 Cor. 6:17).

6. As members of the Body of Christ, we need
to have the consciousness of the Body and a
feeling for the Body; the Body is universal,
the life within us is universal, and the sense
of the Body is universal (Rom. 12:15; 1 Cor.
12:26-27; 2 Cor. 11:28-29).

Day 6

7. The Lord's recovery is to build up Zion—the
reality of the Body of Christ consummating
in the New Jerusalem; in the church life we
must endeavor to reach today's Zion (Eph.
1:22-23; 4:16; 1 Cor. 1:2; 12:27; Rev. 14:1;
21:2).

8. If we would have the reality of the Body of
Christ, we must allow Christ to make His
home in our hearts; the reality of the Body is
the inner experience of the indwelling Christ
(Eph. 3:16-17a; 4:16; Col. 1:27; 3:4, 15).

9. The Lord urgently needs the reality of the
Body of Christ to be expressed in the local
churches; unless there is a substantial
expression of the Body, the Lord Jesus will
not return (Eph. 1:22-23; 4:16; 5:27, 30; Rev.
19:7).

10. The Lord needs the overcomers to carry out
the economy of God to have the Body of
Christ and to destroy His enemy; without
the overcomers, the Body of Christ cannot
be built up, and unless the Body of Christ is
built up, Christ cannot come back for His
bride (Eph. 1:10; 3:10; Rev. 12:11; 19:7-9).

Morning Nourishment

John But as many as received Him, to them He gave the
1:12-13 authority to become children of God, to those who
believe into His name, who were begotten not of
blood, nor of the will of the flesh, nor of the will
of man, but of God.

1 John Beloved, now we are children of God, and it has not
3:2 yet been manifested what we will be. We know that if
He is manifested, we will be like Him because we will
see Him even as He is.

It is only by God's becoming man to make man God that the
Body of Christ can be produced. This point is the high peak of
the vision given to us by God.

God is God, and He Himself has begotten us as His children.
Whatever anything is born of, that is what it is. We cannot say
that when sheep beget sheep, the old sheep are sheep but the little sheep are not sheep. Since God has begotten us, we are the
children of God. Furthermore, 1 John 3 says that God will work on
us to such an extent that we will be like Him completely (v. 2)....
The Lord...shows us clearly that we are God in life and nature. A
father begets a son, and this son surely is the same as the father
in life and nature. Suppose the father is an emperor. We cannot
say that all his children are emperors. The children have only
their father's life and nature but not his status; this is clear. God
did this that He might produce a Body for Christ, that is, that He
might produce an organism for the Triune God, the ultimate
manifestation of which is the New Jerusalem. (*The High Peak of
the Vision and the Reality of the Body of Christ*, pp. 15-16)

Today's Reading

In God's relationship with man we can see that God has a
heart's desire and a purpose; that is, God wants to make Himself
man and to make man God that the two—God and man—may
become altogether the same. God is God, yet He made Himself a
man and lived a human life exactly the same as man in the
human nature and the human life....Man is man, yet God wants

to make man the same as He is, of the same kind and the same likeness as He is in life and in nature, except that we human beings have no share in His person. Thus, His attributes become our human virtues and His glorious image is expressed and lived out through us. Eventually, God and man become a matching pair in the universe. This couple look like man, yet actually they are God. This is truly mysterious to the uttermost. This is God's highest and ultimate purpose in man.

First, God created man in such a way that man had His image outwardly and had a spirit inwardly to contact and receive God. Second, God became a man and accomplished redemption to solve all the problems between God and man and release the divine life. Third, He became the life-giving Spirit....When He as the life-giving Spirit comes into us, He is begotten in us. When He is born in us, we are regenerated to become another person, no longer the original person. Such a person is born of God and has the authority to be a child of God (John 1:12-13). Now we not only are created by God and have His image; we also are born of God. He Himself is born into us to be our life, our person, and our everything. He and we become one entity—God yet man, man yet God. (*The Dispensing, Transformation, and Building of the Processed Divine Trinity in the Believers,* pp. 9-11)

God's eternal economy...is God's plan. For this plan, God made an administrative arrangement...for dispensing Himself through the processed and consummated all-inclusive Spirit into His chosen, regenerated, sanctified, and transformed tripartite men so that they can become God in life and nature yet with no share in His Godhead. Thus they are being constituted to be the Body of Christ and will ultimately be enlarged and built up to be the New Jerusalem as God's eternal and corporate expression. (*The Issue of the Union of the Consummated Spirit of the Triune God and the Regenerated Spirit of the Believers,* pp. 77-78)

Further Reading: The High Peak of the Vision and the Reality of the Body of Christ, chs. 1-2

Enlightenment and inspiration: _____

_____

_____

_____

Morning Nourishment

Rom. ...His Son, who came out of the seed of David accord-
1:3-4 ing to the flesh, who was designated the Son of God
in power according to the Spirit of holiness out of
the resurrection of the dead, Jesus Christ our Lord.
John In that day you will know that I am in My Father,
14:20 and you in Me, and I in you.

Before receiving God's dispensing, we were merely human....
Before incarnation Christ was only divine, but after His incarnation He became a God-man, a man with the divine nature. Now He
is divinely human, and He is also humanly divine. Having been
regenerated by Christ, we have become a part of Him, and now
we are the same as He is—divinely human and humanly divine.

The regenerated ones, who are divinely human and humanly
divine, spontaneously become an organism, the Body of Christ,
which is the church of God as the new man in God's new creation
to carry out God's new "career," that is, to build up the Body of
Christ for the fullness, the expression, of the Triune God. This
fullness as the organism of the Triune God will consummate in
the New Jerusalem. The Bible begins with God in His creation as
the initiation and ends with the New Jerusalem, which is the
mingling of the Triune God and all His chosen, redeemed, regenerated, transformed, conformed, and glorified tripartite people.
The New Jerusalem is thus a constitution of God with man to
express God for eternity. (*Life-study of Job*, p. 58)

Today's Reading

Concerning the first thirty years of the Lord's life on earth, the
Gospels do not say much. However, we can find out that He lived
in a poor carpenter's home, and He was called a carpenter (Matt.
13:55; Mark 6:3). I did not understand, however, what the significance was of the Lord's living the life of a carpenter for thirty
years on the earth. Now...I have seen that He used those thirty-
three and a half years to live out the model of a God-man living.

After His death and resurrection He produced many brothers
who, with Him as the oldest Brother, become the one great man in

the universe. What is this great, universal man? This is a God-man, one who is God yet man and man yet God. (*The High Peak of the Vision and the Reality of the Body of Christ,* p. 46)

The preparation of the dwelling place in John 14 is God becoming man and man becoming God that God and man, man and God, can be joined and mingled together to become a mutual dwelling place. This preparation...requires much building work. On God's side, in order to dwell with man, He Himself had to pass through incarnation, human living, crucifixion, and resurrection. On man's side, in order to dwell with God, man likewise has to pass through regeneration, sanctification, renewing, and transformation. All these are the work of building the dwelling place of God and man so that ultimately God and man can become a mutual dwelling place. (*The Issue of the Union of the Consummated Spirit of the Triune God and the Regenerated Spirit of the Believers,* p. 28)

God builds Himself into man and builds man into Himself. He Himself becomes this constitution with Himself as the intrinsic element—the source, element, and essence within—and with His redeemed people built together in the intrinsic element...to become the framework. This is the one new man in the universe. ...The ultimate consummation of this new man is the New Jerusalem. The New Jerusalem is a constitution of God and man and man and God,...constituted into one; it is divinity expressed in humanity and humanity glorified in divinity. Therefore,...divinity and humanity become a mutual dwelling place. The One who is God yet man dwells in the one who is man yet God, and the one who is man yet God dwells in the One who is God yet man. They are a mutual dwelling place. Thus, His divine glory shines forth radiantly with great splendor in humanity....This economy is God and man becoming one entity, as one who is God yet man and man yet God. (*The Dispensing, Transformation, and Building of the Processed Divine Trinity in the Believers,* p. 38)

Further Reading: The Dispensing, Transformation, and Building of the Processed Divine Trinity in the Believers, chs. 1, 4

Enlightenment and inspiration: _____
_____
_____
_____

Morning Nourishment

John   And when He had said this, He breathed into *them*
20:22 and said to them, Receive the Holy Spirit.
2 Cor. And the Lord is the Spirit; and where the Spirit of the
3:17-18 Lord is, there is freedom. But we all with unveiled face,
       beholding and reflecting like a mirror the glory of the
       Lord, are being transformed into the same image from
       glory to glory, even as from the Lord Spirit.

Christ is now in resurrection as the life-giving Spirit, the consummation of the processed Triune God. Since He is in resurrection, we, His believers, should also be in resurrection and live in resurrection....This is resurrection—the termination of the natural and the germination of the spiritual, to transform the natural into the spiritual. In resurrection we do not live a natural life but a life that was terminated in the old nature and germinated in the new nature to make us members of Christ.

Christ today is a corporate Christ with many members (1 Cor. 12:12). This means that He is not only the Head but the Head with the Body. Here we have the very essence of God's economy, with Christ and His Body as its center and reality.

In this economy God became man in order to make man God in life and nature (but not in the Godhead) through a marvelous process. With God this process was incarnation, human living, death, and resurrection. With us this process is regeneration, sanctification, renewing, transformation, conformation, and glorification. God has become man, and eventually man will become God in life and in nature. Then the eternal economy of God will be accomplished. (*Life-study of 1 & 2 Kings*, p. 145)

Today's Reading

How does God make man God? First, God became a man. The process which God went through from incarnation to resurrection was the procedure for Him to become man. Eventually in His resurrection He became the life-giving Spirit. In this Spirit He comes to carry out the work of making man God. First, He is now the sanctifying Spirit, as we are told in 1 Peter 1:2....We were sanctified before we were saved. Second, at the time we heard the gospel, the Spirit put faith into us. Third, when we believed, the life of God, which is God Himself, Christ Himself, entered into us. Thus we were regenerated.

The sanctification we experience after our regeneration is not positional sanctification but dispositional sanctification. When the Spirit separated us from sinners, that was the positional sanctification that took place before we were saved. When the Spirit comes into us to change our disposition, that is the dispositional sanctification that takes place after our regeneration. This dispositional sanctification is not accomplished in one day. This sanctification issues in renewing, which is a lifelong matter. Renewing issues in transformation, which is also a lifelong matter. The final result of transformation is to be conformed to the image of the Lord and be the same as He is. From the first step of regeneration to the final step of conformation, everything is carried out by the Spirit. Eventually, this Spirit will bring us into glory so that God will be completely expressed from within us through our...body....That is glorification....It is by these steps that God is making us God.

The Lord Jesus resurrected and ascended to the heavens, and He is now in heaven as the life-giving Spirit. This life-giving Spirit is the One who is God yet man, who was incarnated, passed through human living, died, and was resurrected....In His ascension He is the Mediator of the new covenant (Heb. 8:6), the surety of the new covenant (7:22), the High Priest (8:1), and the heavenly Minister (v. 2). Now in the heavens He is doing one thing, that is, to work on all His redeemed and regenerated people to make them God. How does He do it? He does it by being in them to continuously sanctify them, renew them, and transform them. This transformation is to deify them. (*The High Peak of the Vision and the Reality of the Body of Christ*, pp. 42-43, 47-48)

Further Reading: The High Peak of the Vision and the Reality of the Body of Christ, ch. 3; Life-study of 1 & 2 Kings, msg. 21

Enlightenment and inspiration: _____

_____
_____
_____

Morning Nourishment

Gal. 2:20 I am crucified with Christ; and *it is* no longer I *who* live, but *it is* Christ *who* lives in me; and the *life* which I now live in the flesh I live in faith, the *faith* of the Son of God, who loved me and gave Himself up for me.

Phil. 3:10-11 To know Him and the power of His resurrection and the fellowship of His sufferings, being conformed to His death, if perhaps I may attain to the out-resurrection from the dead.

The highest peak in God's economy [is] the reality of the Body of Christ. We know the term *the Body of Christ*. We may even have seen the revelation of the Body of Christ. Yet we have to admit that...we can see very little of the reality of the Body of Christ within us and among us. I am speaking not of the revelation, not even of the vision, but of the reality of the Body of Christ.

This reality has nothing to do with any kind of organization or with anything which remains in the nature of organization. Also, the reality of the Body of Christ is not a system in any way, because no system is organic. The reality of the Body of Christ is absolutely and altogether organic. (*The Practical Points concerning Blending*, p. 30)

Today's Reading

The Body of Christ is not merely a term but a reality. The reality of the Body of Christ is the union and mingling of God with man to live out a corporate God-man. For this we need to pass through death and resurrection, dying daily and being resurrected daily. We also need to be in the Spirit and walk according to the Spirit daily.

Let me speak something of my own experience. For many years I have felt that I am quite all right, but recently the Lord showed me differently....It is according to moral standards that I do not do bad things or speak bad words to my wife. Yet, I do not take God as my Husband and speak by Him. I myself am the husband, and I speak by myself and speak concerning the work by myself. Recently, because of the great vision that I saw, I have been practicing one thing, that is, when I am going to speak to others, within me I ask, "Is it you who want to speak, or is it your Husband?" In other words, "Is it you who want to speak, or is it the Spirit who dwells in you? Is your speaking in the Spirit and according to the Spirit?" If we use this standard to weigh or measure ourselves, we will see that we are far below the standard. Although we have seen the vision concerning the Body of Christ and can speak clearly about it, what we have as the reality of the Body of Christ is very little. (*The High Peak of the Vision and the Reality of the Body of Christ,* pp. 54-55)

In Philippians 3 Paul said that he lived a life conformed to the death of Christ (v. 10)....His old life was conformed to the image of the death of Christ by the power of Christ's resurrection. The power of resurrection strengthened him to live the life of a God-man. The Lord expects that many of us would be such ones.... Such a corporate living is the reality of the Body of Christ, dear saints. This is a corporate living of the conformity to the death of Christ through the power of the resurrection of Christ. (*The Practical Points concerning Blending,* pp. 36-37)

The God-created humanity was very good, but it did not have anything of God's nature. It was only human, without divinity.... In His redemption God destroyed the fallen part, rescued the God-created part, and then dispensed Himself into this redeemed humanity....God's redemption includes not only death but also resurrection. Without resurrection, God could not bring back to Himself the lost created man....In resurrection God used His own life, nature, and element as the substance to uplift the redeemed created man...[and] put Himself into man. Now this man is regenerated and uplifted, having all that God is within him. The entire God has entered into this resurrected, regenerated, and uplifted man. This man is what the Bible calls the new man (Eph. 4:24). (*Life-study of Proverbs,* p. 56)

Further Reading: The High Peak of the Vision and the Reality of the Body of Christ, ch. 4; *The Practical Points concerning Blending,* ch. 4

Enlightenment and inspiration: _____

_____

_____

_____

Morning Nourishment

1 Cor. For even as the body is one and has many members,
12:12-13 yet all the members of the body, being many, are one
body, so also is the Christ. For also in one Spirit we
were all baptized into one Body, whether Jews or
Greeks, whether slaves or free, and were all given to
drink one Spirit.
26-27 And whether one member suffers, all the members
suffer with *it;* or one member is glorified, all the
members rejoice with *it.* Now you are the Body of
Christ, and members individually.

To know the Body is the proper recovery of the Lord. If we are
for the recovery, we need to realize what the recovery is. The Lord
desires to recover the missed Body of Christ and to recover the
neglected oneness of the Body of Christ. This is the Lord's recovery. (*The Problems Causing the Turmoils in the Church Life,* p. 31)

Today's Reading

We need to see that God's economy as God's plan, His administration, is to create, to constitute, and to produce a Body for His
Son. This is the major purpose of God's economy. Christ gained
this Body, which is a part of Himself, His counterpart. Adam living alone typifies Christ being alone before He had gained His
counterpart, His Body, the church. God said it was not good for
Adam to be alone. So God made him fall into a deep sleep, opened
his side, and took out a rib. Genesis 2 says that God built a woman
with that rib (v. 22). This indicates that Eve came out of Adam.
After being built up, Eve was brought back to Adam, and God
made these two into one flesh. Ephesians 5 tells us that this is a
type of the great mystery of Christ and the church (vv. 31-32). This
type will be fulfilled in the New Jerusalem, which is the wife of
the Lamb (Rev. 21:2). This is the goal of God's economy. (*The Problems Causing the Turmoils in the Church Life,* p. 25)

Corporately, the many sons of God are the church; organically,
they are the Body of Christ. The Body of Christ is the church, the
house of God, the kingdom of God, and the bride, the counterpart,

of Christ. In each aspect, the church takes the Body of Christ as its organic factor. Without the Body of Christ, the church is lifeless and is a mere human organization. Without the Body of Christ,...there cannot be the house of God, which is constituted with the children born of God the Father, and there cannot be the kingdom of God, which is the realm of God's life. Without the life of Christ, there also cannot be the bride of Christ who, as His counterpart, must match Him to be a couple with Him....The church as the house of God, the kingdom of God, and the bride of Christ takes the Body of Christ as its organic factor. (*The Governing and Controlling Vision in the Bible,* pp. 22-23)

Whenever we do something, we must have a proper consideration for the Body. We need to consider how the Body would feel about what we are doing. The biggest problem, the unique problem, is not knowing the Body and not caring for the Body. If we take care of the Body and are concerned for the Body, there will be no problems. We are here for the Body. Without the backing of the Body, without the backing of the recovery, we have no way to practice the local churches. If we practice the local church life and neglect the view of the Body, our local church becomes a local sect.

The recovery is for the Body, not for any individual or merely for any individual local church. If we are going to do something, we have to consider how the Body, the recovery, will react. The problems are all due to the lack of seeing the Body and of caring for the Body. We all need to come back to the truth, and to practice the truth is to take care of the Body. Sometimes the Body is strong, and sometimes the Body is weak, but it is still the Body. If we come back to the truth and take care of the proper order in the Body, the Body will immediately become stronger. All the problems are due to one thing: not seeing, not knowing, and not caring for the Body. We have to honor the Body. (*The Problems Causing the Turmoils in the Church Life,* p. 35)

Further Reading: The Problems Causing the Turmoils in the Church Life, chs. 3-4; *The Governing and Controlling Vision in the Bible,* ch. 2

Enlightenment and inspiration: _____

_____

_____

_____

Morning Nourishment

Eph. That He would grant you, according to the riches of
3:16-17 His glory, to be strengthened with power through His
Spirit into the inner man, that Christ may make
His home in your hearts through faith...
Col. And let the peace of Christ arbitrate in your hearts,
3:15 to which also you were called in one Body; and be
thankful.
Rev. Let us rejoice and exult, and let us give the glory to
19:7 Him, for the marriage of the Lamb has come, and His
wife has made herself ready.

We must see what the church is. The church is the Body, and
there is only one Body. You need light and revelation to see that
the church is the Body. On the earth today there is Christianity, but
that is not the Body. There are those who love the Lord, but that is
not the Body. There are those who are well-cultivated, but that
is not the Body. There are those who pursue spirituality, but that is
not the Body. What the Lord wants today is...the Body. There
is only one Body. Brothers and sisters, I can assure you that,
unless there is a substantial expression of the Body, the Lord
Jesus will never return. The Lord said, "I come quickly," but He
has not yet returned. Why? Because the Body is not here; because
the Body has not yet been manifested on the earth. (*One Body,
One Spirit, and One New Man*, pp. 14-15)

Today's Reading

Ephesians 3:17 tells us that Christ is now making His home in
our hearts. In John 14:23 the Lord said, "If anyone loves Me...My
Father will love him, and We will come to him and make an abode
with him." This word *make* is not a small word. To make is to build.
The only way to make a home is by building. This building is not by
anything physical but by the spiritual element and spiritual
essence of the Divine Trinity. This building actually is a kind of
organic constitution. The reality of the Body of Christ is a living by
all the God-men united, joined, and constituted together with God
by mingling humanity with divinity and divinity with humanity.

In John 14:17-20 the Lord told us that by the Spirit of reality
coming into us the Lord would live....This means that when the
Spirit of reality comes, the Lord Himself would dwell in us in
order to live in us. He said, "Because I live, you also shall live"
(v. 19b). He lives and we live....This is not a kind of individual living. This is a corporate living that we live with the Lord since He
lives within us....The eternal God, after His creation and after
passing through the necessary processes, eventually became the
Spirit of reality...[in order to live] in us that we may live together
with Him. So this living is a mingling.

For us to reach the high peak of God's economy, that is, the
reality of the Body of Christ, we must firstly see this divine
indwelling within us....I do not believe anyone among us, including me, is constantly and instantly living with the indwelling
Lord.

We are God-men who are doing things and having our being
not only according to God's heart but also according to the Spirit
who has been processed and consummated through death and
resurrection. We need to check whether or not we are doing
everything in the Spirit and having our being according to such a
Spirit.

The reality of the Body of Christ is the aggregate, the totality,
of such a living by a group of God-men. This kind of a living, which
is the reality of the Body of Christ, will close this age, the age of
the church, and will bring Christ back to take, possess, and rule
over this earth with these God-men in the kingdom age. They
were perfected, completed, and consummated in the church age.
So in the next age, the kingdom age, they will reign with Christ
for a thousand years (Rev. 20:4-6).

Today in the church age, the God-men who were perfected and
matured are Zion, the overcomers, the vital groups within the
churches. (*The Practical Points concerning Blending,* pp. 26, 40-
41, 44-45)

Further Reading: The Practical Points concerning Blending, chs. 1-3, 5

Enlightenment and inspiration: _____

_____

_____

_____

What Miracle! What Mystery!

1   What miracle! What mystery!
    That God and man should blended be!
    God became man to make man God,
    Untraceable economy!
    From His good pleasure, heart's desire,
    His highest goal attained will be.

2   Flesh He became, the first God-man,
    His pleasure that I God may be:
    In life and nature I'm God's kind,
    Though Godhead's His exclusively.
    His attributes my virtues are;
    His glorious image shines through me.

3   No longer I alone that live,
    But God together lives with me.
    Built with the saints in the Triune God,
    His universal house we'll be,
    And His organic Body we
    For His expression corp'rately.

4   Jerusalem, the ultimate,
    Of visions the totality;
    The Triune God, tripartite man—
    A loving pair eternally—
    As man yet God they coinhere,
    A mutual dwelling place to be;
    God's glory in humanity
    Shines forth in splendor radiantly!

Composition for prophecy with main point and sub-points: _____

_____

_____

_____

_____

_____

_____

_____

_____

_____

_____

_____

_____

_____

_____

_____

_____

_____

_____

_____

_____

_____

_____

_____

_____

_____

_____

_____

_____

_____

_____

_____

_____

_____

_____

Honoring Christ as the Head and
Living in the Divine and Mystical Realm

Scripture Reading: Eph. 1:22-23; Col. 1:18; 2:19; Gal. 3:14; Rom. 8:9; 2 Cor. 3:17-18

Day 1
&
Day 2

I. **We need to honor Christ as the unique Head of the Body by holding Him as the Head (Eph. 1:22-23; Col. 1:18; 2:19):**

A. In Christ's ascension God inaugurated Him into the headship of the universe; the Head of the whole universe is Jesus (Acts 2:36; Eph. 1:22-23; Phil. 2:9-11).

B. The Head is a matter of authority; for Christ to be the Head means that He has the authority in the Body (Matt. 28:18):

1. Holding the Head means that only Christ is the Head; holding the Head is to come absolutely under His authority (Eph. 4:15).

2. Honoring Christ as the Head involves a repudiation of all other heads.

3. The place of all the members is to hold the Head and to acknowledge Him as the unique and supreme authority in all things (Col. 1:18; 2:19).

4. Christ is the Head of the Body, and life can flow freely to us only when He is in full control (Rev. 22:1).

5. For the Body to hold the Head means that the Body does not allow itself to be separated from the Head (Col. 2:19).

C. The Body comes into existence from the transmission of the Head, and the Body is one with the Head in the divine life and in the divine nature (Eph. 1:22-23).

Day 3

D. The members of the Body are fitted together and are able to live the Body life through holding the Head (4:15-16; Col. 2:19):

1. Our relationship with the Head determines

our relationship to the other members; it is our common relationship to Him that causes us to be related to one another.

2. When we do not hold the Head, our fellowship becomes invalid; the basis of our fellowship is our mutual holding of the Head (Acts 2:42; 1 John 1:3).

3. We have no direct communion one with another; it is all through the Head (Col. 1:18):

   a. Forming parties means that a few Christians have a direct relationship with one another and are detached from the authority of the Head; they communicate with each other directly, but their communication has not passed through the Head.

   b. We must not move in relation to another member except under the direction of the Head.

Day 4

4. To live the Body life, we must be under the Head and take the Head as the life, the principal object, and the center (Eph. 4:15-16):

   a. To have the Body life, whatever we think or do has to be under the control of Christ as the Head; we have to take Him as the center of our whole being.

   b. We have to coordinate with all the members to live a life that expresses the Head (Rom. 12:5).

E. We need to be subject to one another in the fear of Christ, who is the Head (Eph. 5:21, 23):

   1. Not being subject to one another offends Christ as the Head and means that we have no fear of Christ in His headship (v. 23; 1:22).

   2. Actually, not being subject to one another is rebellion against the Head.

   3. Only the Head is superior, and only the Head should be unique and different from

the Body; none of the members is in a special or super class.

Day 5

II. We need to live in the divine and mystical realm of the consummated Spirit and the pneumatic Christ (Gal. 3:14; Rom. 8:9; 2 Cor. 3:17-18):

A. The Triune God Himself is a divine and mystical realm; the three of the Divine Trinity are self-existing, ever-existing, coexisting, and coinhering, and as such, the Father, the Son, and the Spirit are a divine and mystical realm (John 14:10-11; Matt. 28:19; 2 Cor. 13:14).

B. The divine and mystical realm into which we may enter is the divine and mystical realm of the consummated Spirit and the pneumatic Christ; we should learn to live in this realm (Phil. 1:19; Rom. 8:9; 2 Cor. 13:14; Gal. 3:14).

C. In the divine and mystical realm we receive the transmission of the ascended Christ and the supply of His heavenly ministry (Eph. 1:22; Heb. 8:1-2).

Day 6

D. In the divine and mystical realm we experience God's organic salvation (Rom. 5:10).

E. In the divine and mystical realm we live in the kingdom of God as the realm of the divine species (John 3:3, 5).

F. In the divine and mystical realm we live in divine fellowship; this is the reality of living in the Body of Christ (1 John 1:3, 7; Acts 2:42; Rom. 12:5).

G. In the divine and mystical realm we are mingled with the Triune God for the keeping of the oneness (John 17:21; Eph. 4:3-6):

1. The genuine oneness is in the Triune God (John 17:21):

a. The genuine oneness of the believers is actually the oneness of the Triune God.

b. It is only in the Triune God that we can be perfected into one (v. 23).

2. The genuine oneness is the mingling of the believers with the Triune God (Eph. 3:14—4:6):

   a. To have this oneness we must be in the Triune God as the divine and mystical realm.

   b. The believers are one with the Triune God in the divine and mystical realm of the consummated Spirit and the pneumatic Christ (Gal. 3:14; Rom. 8:9; 2 Cor. 3:17-18).

H. The Body of Christ is in the divine and mystical realm; the more we are in the reality of the Body of Christ, the more we are in the divine and mystical realm (Rom. 12:4-5; 1 Cor. 12:12-13, 27; Eph. 1:22-23; 4:16).

I. If we would live in the divine and mystical realm, we need to have a vision of this realm, appreciate this realm, consider highly the entry into this realm, walk by the Spirit and according to the spirit, experience the dividing of soul and spirit, and exercise to be one spirit with the Lord (John 3:3; Eph. 1:17-18; 2:18; Gal. 5:16; Rom. 8:4; Heb. 4:12; 1 Cor. 6:17; 2 Tim. 1:7).

Morning Nourishment

Acts Therefore let all the house of Israel know assuredly
2:36 that God has made Him both Lord and Christ, this
Jesus whom you have crucified.
Phil. ...God highly exalted Him and bestowed on Him
2:9-11 the name which is above every name, that in the
name of Jesus every knee should bow, of those who
are in heaven and on earth and under the earth,
and every tongue should openly confess that Jesus
Christ is Lord to the glory of God the Father.

Because Christ gained the human element in His incarnation
and accomplished God's purpose and defeated God's enemy in
His crucifixion, He is now fully qualified to be the Head of the universe in God's administration.

After Christ's crucifixion He rested for three days....After resting in the tomb for three days, Christ resurrected and then
ascended into the heavens. In His ascension He was inaugurated
into the full headship of the entire universe. In the third heavens
Christ was given to be Head over all things to the church. Christ
is also the head of every man (1 Cor. 11:3a). Thus, in His ascension
Christ's headship was fully established. (*Crucial Principles for
the Christian Life and the Church Life,* p. 71)

Today's Reading

Christ's headship was not fully established until His ascension, because He needed to become a man and be crucified in
order to accomplish God's eternal purpose and to defeat and
destroy God's enemy. This truth is in the Bible, yet if we do not
have the light, we will not be able to see it. Because the human
mentality can only know doctrine, we need heavenly light, vision,
and revelation in order to see a vision of the truth. We need to
repeat this truth again and again until our inner eyes are opened
and we see it. Once Christ picked up humanity through incarnation and was crucified to accomplish God's eternal purpose and
defeat and destroy God's enemy, He was qualified both in element
and in achievement to be the Head over all things. Thus, in His

ascension God inaugurated Him into the universal headship over all things for God's administration. Today the headship of Christ is fully established. (*Crucial Principles for the Christian Life and the Church Life,* pp. 71-72)

Christ was made Lord and Christ by God (Acts 2:36). As God, the Lord was the Lord all the time (Luke 1:43; John 11:21; 20:28). However, in His incarnation He became a man; the Creator became a creature. As man, He was made the Lord in His ascension after He brought His humanity into God in His resurrection. Moreover, as God's sent and anointed One, He was Christ from the time He was born (Luke 2:11; Matt. 1:16; John 1:41; Matt. 16:16), but as such a One, He was officially made the very Christ of God in His ascension.

God made the man Jesus the Lord to head up and own all things....Only Christ Jesus is the Lord. As Christians we have the deep realization that Jesus is our Lord. Especially during times of trouble or even at times when something good happens to us, the first thing we often say is, "O Lord!" How good it is to have Jesus as Lord! Jesus was made the Lord, as the Lord of all (Acts 10:36), to possess all. If one does not have Jesus, he does not have an owner. Jesus was also made the Christ in His resurrection and ascension to carry out God's commission, His plan and eternal economy. The Lord is the Owner, and Christ is the Doer. He is the One who owns all things, and He is the One who fulfills God's commission. (*Leadership in the New Testament,* p. 43)

Paul, the greatest apostle, received orders directly from Christ the Head, and we, the smallest members, also receive orders directly from Christ the Head. This honors the Head. The headship of Christ does not allow for there to be any other heads or subheads. Any other head is an insult to Christ. Therefore, in the church there is no head other than Christ. (*Crucial Principles for the Christian Life and the Church Life,* p. 78)

Further Reading: Crucial Principles for the Christian Life and the Church Life, ch. 6; *Leadership in the New Testament,* chs. 3-4

Enlightenment and inspiration: _____

_____

_____

_____

Morning Nourishment

Matt. And Jesus came and spoke to them, saying, All author-
28:18 ity has been given to Me in heaven and on earth.
Eph. But holding to truth in love, we may grow up into
4:15 Him in all things, who is the Head, Christ.
Col. And He is the Head of the Body, the church; He is the
1:18 beginning, the Firstborn from the dead, that He Himself might have the first place in all things.

What do Christ being the Head of the church and the church
being the Body of Christ mean? They mean that all authority is in
Him. All authority is in Him because all life is in Him. The whole
Body is consummated in Him; He is the fountainhead of the life of
the Body. The Body has no life of its own. "God gave to us eternal
life and this life is in His Son" (1 John 5:11). Even after eternal life
is given to us, it still rests in His Son. The Son does not part with
it; He retains it in Himself. "He who has the Son has the life"
(v. 12). This verse does not say, "He who has the life has the life."
We do not possess life as life; only by possessing the Son do we
have life. A Christian receives his life from the Lord. Yet this life
can never be separated from the Lord. A believer is related not
just to life. By being related to this life, a believer is related to the
Son of God. This life makes us members of the Body of Christ.
This life relationship rules out the possibility of being separated
from the Head, because our life is derived from the Head.
(Watchman Nee, *The Mystery of Christ*, pp. 31-32)

Today's Reading

The flow of life in us continually depends upon our relationship to the Son. As soon as there is any obstruction in our fellowship with Him, the life in us is immediately blocked. He is the
Head of the Body, and life can flow freely to us only when He is in
full control.

The power of our existence is derived from Christ. This is why
we cannot do anything independently. Only the Lord is our Head,
and only He has the authority to direct the moves of the members
of His Body. In this age of lawlessness, any suggestion of the need

of authority is unwelcome; but if we are to understand and enter into the life of the Body, we must know the authority of the Head. My hand can do nothing without direction from the head. The head must command if the members are to move. Christ is the life of the Body, and Christ is also the authority in the Body. All the moves of the members of His Body must be under the direction of the Head. For Christ to be the Head means that He has the authority in the Body. We are not the head, and we do not have the authority. The only thing we should do is submit to the authority of the Lord....In the Body of Christ, no individual's idea or proposal counts; all these have to be cast down. We should only submit to the authority of the Head. We should just listen to His command and do as He says.

An acceptance of Christ as Head involves a repudiation of all other heads. Christ alone is the Head of the Body; no one else can be the head. You cannot be the head, nor can anyone in the church be the head, because there can only be one Head in the Body; there cannot be two heads. Only Christ is the Head. Therefore, all of us have to obey Christ....If we desire to live in the Body of Christ, we have to learn to submit to the authority of our Lord Jesus. Anyone who cannot submit, who always expresses his opinions and proposals, and who insists on being the head has never seen the Body. Once a man realizes that he is a member in the Body, there will surely be a feeling of submission in him because submission is a law of the Body.

Paul spoke of "holding the Head, out from whom all the Body, being richly supplied and knit together by means of the joints and sinews, grows with the growth of God" (Col. 2:19). Since Christ is the Head of the Body, we have to hold the Head. Holding the Head is acknowledging that only Christ is the Head; it is coming absolutely under His authority. (Watchman Nee, *The Mystery of Christ,* pp. 32-33)

Further Reading: The Mystery of Christ, ch. 6; Crucial Principles for the Christian Life and the Church Life, ch. 7

Enlightenment and inspiration: _____

_____

_____

_____

Morning Nourishment

Eph. And He subjected all things under His feet and gave
1:22-23 Him *to be* Head over all things to the church, which
is His Body, the fullness of the One who fills all in all.
Col. ...Holding the Head, out from whom all the Body,
2:19 being richly supplied and knit together by means of
the joints and sinews, grows with the growth of God.

Humanity is the center of God's creation. The heading up of all
things in Christ takes place as the Triune God works Himself into
man as the center of His creation. According to Ephesians 1:22,
God has subjected all things under the feet of the resurrected and
ascended Christ and "gave Him to be Head over all things to the
church." The little word "to" is very important because it implies a
kind of transmission. Whatever Christ, the Head, has attained and
obtained is now being transmitted to His Body, the church. By
means of this transmission, the church shares with Christ all His
attainments. The church shares in His resurrection from among
the dead, His being seated in His transcendency, the subjection of
all things under His feet, and His headship over all things. As the
element of Christ is transmitted into the church, all that He has accomplished, attained, and obtained is transfused into the church as
well. Through this marvelous transmission we become the Body of
Christ, the fullness of the One who fills all in all. Then, as His Body,
we shall become the means by which God will head up all things in
Christ. The crucial factor here is the divine transmission, the trans-
fusion of Christ into our being. (*Life-study of Ephesians*, p. 810)

Today's Reading

We can be joined to the brothers and sisters only when we hold
the Head. The members of the Body are fitted together and able
to live the Body life through holding the Head. Our relationship to
the Head determines our relationship to the other members.
All the questions regarding our relationship with the brothers
and sisters can only be solved when we come under the absolute
authority of the Lord. Unless we recognize the headship of Christ
in the Body, we will never have a perfect fellowship with the other

members, because it is our common relationship to Him that causes us to be related to one another....Apart from Christ, we have no means of fellowship. When we do not hold the Head, our fellowship becomes invalid. The basis of our fellowship is our mutual holding of the Head. When we all hold the Head, we will hold to one another, and our relationship with the Body will be proper.

If we hold the Head, we cannot have a special relationship, feeling, or fellowship with any individual or group of individuals. There is no room for our own preferences in the Body. We have no direct communion one with another; it is all through the Head. For instance, when my left hand hurts, my right hand comes to its aid immediately. The right hand does this because both the left hand and the right hand are under the direction of the head. The mutual relationship of the members passes through the Head first....Forming parties means that a few Christians have a direct relationship with one another and are detached from the authority of the Head. They communicate with each other directly, but their communication has not passed through the Head. They have a special relationship with one another, but their relationship has not passed through the Head.

We must not move in relation to another member except under the direction of the Lord. If He asks us to do something for a fellow member and the fellow member does not appreciate it, we do not need to worry since all of our dealings are with the Head. If we hold the Head, getting all our direction from Him and doing all as unto Him, we do not need to worry about the consequences.

In the church we all must hold the Head, whether it involves the understanding of the truth, the handling of business, or any other matter. Christ is the unique authority in the Body. The place of all the members is to hold the Head and to acknowledge Him as the unique and supreme authority in all things. (Watchman Nee, *The Mystery of Christ,* pp. 33-35)

Further Reading: Life-study of Ephesians, msg. 96; *Life-study of Colossians,* msg. 56

Enlightenment and inspiration: _____

_____

_____

_____

Morning Nourishment

Eph.   ...The Head, Christ, out from whom all the Body, being
4:15-16 joined together and being knit together through every
         joint of the rich supply and *through* the operation in
         the measure of each one part, causes the growth of the
         Body unto the building up of itself in love.
5:21   Being subject to one another in the fear of Christ.

To live in the Body is to live corporately with the members
under the Head (Col. 1:18). To live the Body life, first we must
be under the Head and take the Head as the life, the principal
object, and the center (Eph. 4:15-16). Many people desire to be
holy, spiritual, and overcoming. But these are their own desires.
They are not under Christ the Head. Instead they are their own
head. This makes them unable to live the Body life. To have the
Body life, whatever we think or do has to be under the control of
Christ the Head; we have to take Him as the center of our whole
being. Second, we have to coordinate with all the members to live
a life that expresses the Head (Rom. 12:5). We have to learn to
live in the Body and submit to the Head all the time, to care for
the feeling of the Body, and to live together with all the members.
We should not take our own spirituality, holiness, or victory as the
center. This will make us particular and individualistic and will
cause us to condemn others and make demands on them. Neither
should we try to keep some regulations and conform ourselves to
others. Rather, we should live in the Spirit to express Christ in an
organic and coordinated way. (*The Oneness and the One Accord
according to the Lord's Aspiration and the Body Life and Service
according to His Pleasure*, p. 39)

Today's Reading

The constitution of the church is according to the fact that
Christ is the unique Head. There is no other leader. Regardless of
how great our gift or our commission from the Lord is, we are all
only members, not leaders. No one among us should accept anyone
as an official, unique, or permanent leader. In carrying things out,
there is the need for leadership. The Bible shows that on the day of

Pentecost there was the need for someone to rise up to declare the gospel to the people. Peter took the lead to meet this need, but he was not an official, permanent, organizational, or positional leader. His leadership was instant and depended on his present spiritual capacity. At that time Peter had the greatest capacity; therefore, he spontaneously took the lead to carry out that ministry. However, when he later became weak, another one was raised up to accomplish God's purpose. The leadership in the Lord's recovery today must be the same....By practicing in this way, we will have no official or permanent leader among us. We have only one Leader—Christ. (*Crucial Principles for the Christian Life and the Church Life*, p. 80)

To keep a pleasant, good, and beautiful order in the recovery, we need to be subject to one another in the fear of Christ (Eph. 5:21). Not only should the younger ones be subject to the older ones, but also the older ones should be subject to the younger ones (1 Pet. 5:5). The elders should not be a special class in the church. Peter charges them not to lord it over the church (v. 3). On the other hand, the saints should respect the elders....The wives should respect the husbands, and the husbands should also respect the wives. Our subjection with respect is a mutual thing.

Not being subject to one another offends Christ as the Head. Actually, not being subject to one another is rebellion against the Head. This means that we have no fear of Christ in His headship. Paul tells us that we need to be subject to one another in the fear of Christ, who is the Head. Only the Head is superior. Only the Head should be unique and different from the Body. None of the members, even the apostle Paul, is in a special or super class. (*Elders' Training, Book 11: The Eldership and the God-ordained Way (3)*, p. 129)

Further Reading: The Oneness and the One Accord according to the Lord's Aspiration and the Body Life and Service according to His Pleasure, ch. 3; Elders' Training, Book 11: The Eldership and the God-ordained Way (3), ch. 13

Enlightenment and inspiration: _____

_____

_____

_____

Morning Nourishment

John 14:10-11 Do you not believe that I am in the Father and the Father is in Me? The words that I say to you I do not speak from Myself, but the Father who abides in Me does His works. Believe Me that I am in the Father and the Father is in Me; but if not, believe because of the works themselves.

2 Cor. 13:14 The grace of the Lord Jesus Christ and the love of God and the fellowship of the Holy Spirit be with you all.

[Now] we come to a high peak—the divine and the mystical realm. Something that is mystical is not only spiritual but is also mysterious....The Triune God, the Father, the Son, and the Spirit, is self-existing, ever-existing, and coinhering, with the three of the Divine Trinity dwelling in one another. According to John 14:10 and 11 the Son is in the Father, and the Father is in the Son. This indicates that the Father is embodied in the Son and the Son is the Father's embodiment, forming a divine and mystical realm, the realm of the Triune God. Therefore, the Triune God Himself is a divine and mystical realm.

The divine and mystical realm into which we may enter today is actually not simply the divine and mystical realm of the Triune God but the divine and mystical realm of the consummated Spirit and the pneumatic Christ. (*The Divine and Mystical Realm,* p. 36)

Today's Reading

We have seen that the Spirit has been consummated and that Christ has become the life-giving Spirit, the pneumatic Christ. Thus, we may now speak of the divine and mystical realm of this consummated Spirit and of this pneumatic Christ. What a marvelous realm this is!

The three of the Divine Trinity are self-existing, ever-existing, and coinhering, and as such the Father, the Son, and the Spirit are a divine and mystical realm....God wanted us to be in Him. If He were merely the Triune God without Christ's humanity, death, and resurrection, and we could enter into Him, we would find the

Father, the Son, and the Spirit, but nothing of humanity, death, and resurrection. However, when we enter into the divine and mystical realm of the consummated Spirit and the pneumatic Christ, we have not only divinity but also the humanity of Christ, the death of Christ with its effectiveness, and the resurrection of Christ with its repelling power. Everything is here in this wonderful realm.

Although I was born in China and have become a naturalized American citizen, I can testify that I do not have the feeling that I am either Chinese or American. My realm is not China or America—my realm is the...Triune God. I am here with the Father, with the Son, who was crucified and resurrected, and with the consummated Spirit. Since I am in such a Triune God, I have whatever I need. If I need crucifixion, I find that in this realm I have been crucified already. If I need resurrection, in this realm I have been resurrected already. Praise the Lord for such a divine and mystical realm!

In John 14:20 the Lord Jesus spoke of "that day." "That day" was the day of His resurrection (20:19), the day on which He became the pneumatized Christ, the pneumatic Christ.

Let us now read all of verse 20: "In that day you will know that I am in My Father, and you in Me, and I in you." This refers to the divine and mystical realm where not only the Father, the Son, and the Spirit are but also where the believers are. Praise the Lord that, as believers in Christ, we are now in the divine, mystical realm of the consummated Spirit and the pneumatic Christ!

We all need to enter into the divine and mystical realm, not of the Triune God, but of the consummated Spirit and the pneumatic Christ (Phil. 1:19; Rom. 8:9; 2 Cor. 3:17-18).

The Lord Jesus said that when the Spirit of reality came, He would guide the disciples, who would then be in the Spirit of Christ's resurrection, into all the reality concerning God's economy for the Body of Christ, who is the pneumatic Christ and the consummated Spirit. (*The Divine and Mystical Realm,* pp. 40, 44-45)

Further Reading: The Divine and Mystical Realm, chs. 1-2

Enlightenment and inspiration: _____

_____

_____

_____

Morning Nourishment

John
17:21
That they all may be one; even as You, Father, are in Me and I in You, that they also may be in Us; that the world may believe that You have sent Me.

Eph.
3:18-19
[That you] may be full of strength to apprehend with all the saints what the breadth and length and height and depth are and to know the knowledge-surpassing love of Christ, that you may be filled unto all the fullness of God.

All that the Father has is the Son's possession, embodied in the Son....All that the Son possesses is received by the Spirit, realized by the Spirit who became the life-giving Spirit in the resurrection of Christ for the realization of the pneumatic Christ.... The Spirit receives all that Christ has and declares to the disciples (who were then in the reality of Christ's resurrection and in the divine and mystical realm of the pneumatic Christ) for the producing of the assemblies which issue in the Body of Christ that consummates the New Jerusalem to express the all-inclusive Christ for His glorification in eternity (John 16:14-15)....This is the divine transition for the eternal economy of the Divine Trinity. (*The Divine and Mystical Realm,* p. 46)

Today's Reading

All the believers should be in this divine and mystical realm of the consummated Spirit to be mingled with the Triune God for the keeping of oneness.

All the believers should abide in the Son that the Son may abide in them that they may bear much fruit for the glorification (expression) of the Father (15:4-5, 8). In chapter fourteen the Lord prepared the places, the abodes. In chapter fifteen we need to abide in Him as our abode that He may abide in us as His abode.

All the believers should be one, even as the Father is in the Son and the Son in the Father, that they also may be in both the Father and the Son. The Son is in the believers and the Father is in the Son, that the believers may be perfected into one (17:21, 23). Our oneness must be the same as the oneness among the three of the Triune God. Actually, the believers' oneness is the oneness of the Triune God. It is in the Triune God that we can be perfected to be one. The real oneness, therefore, is in the Triune God.

In John 14—16 the Lord Jesus presented a message to His disciples, and then in John 17 He prayed to the Father. In His concluding prayer He indicated that our oneness should be in the Triune God, with the pneumatic Christ and the consummated Spirit. This oneness, which is the genuine oneness, is the mingling of the believers with the Triune God. To have such a oneness the believers must be in the Triune God as a divine and mystical realm. Here the Father is in the Son, the Son is in the believers, and the believers are in the Son, who is in the Father. This means that the believers are one with the Triune God in the divine and mystical realm of the pneumatic Christ and the consummated Spirit.

Christ's heavenly ministry is carried out in this mystical realm, and God's organic salvation is practically accomplished in this realm. If we are not in this realm, we cannot participate in Christ's heavenly ministry or enjoy God's organic salvation.

The believers must consider highly the entry into this realm, realizing that without Christ becoming the life-giving Spirit, without Christ being the pneumatic Christ, without Christ being the Lord Spirit, and without Christ being the Christ in resurrection and not only in the flesh, there is absolutely no way for the believers to participate in, experience, and enjoy the organic section of God's complete salvation in Christ.

What the recovery will be depends upon what [the co-workers and elders] will be.... [This age] is an age of ignorance, a time when Christians are being blinded and held back by traditional theology. Therefore, I am burdened to tell you that you need to enter into a realm, a sphere, a kingdom, which is much higher than the realm you are in now. This higher realm is the mystical realm of Christ's heavenly ministry. (*The Divine and Mystical Realm*, pp. 46-48, 24-25)

Further Reading: The Divine and Mystical Realm, ch. 3; The Breaking of the Outer Man and the Release of the Spirit, pp. 83-92

Enlightenment and inspiration: _____
_____
_____
_____

Hymns, #608

1   What mystery, the Father, Son, and Spirit,
     In person three, in substance all are one.
   How glorious, this God our being enters
     To be our all, thru Spirit in the Son!

     The Triune God has now become our all!
       How wonderful! How glorious!
     This Gift divine we never can exhaust!
       How excellent! How marvelous!

2   How rich the source, the Father as the fountain,
     And all this wealth He wants man to enjoy!
   O blessed fact, this vast, exhaustless portion
     Is now for us forever to employ!

3   How wonderful, the Son is God's expression
     Come in the flesh to dwell with all mankind!
   Redemption's work, how perfectly effective,
     That sinners we with God might oneness find.

4   The Spirit is the Son's transfiguration
     Come into us as life the full supply.
   Amazing fact, our spirit with the Spirit
     Now mingles and in oneness joins thereby!

5   How real it is that God is now the Spirit
     For us to touch, experience day by day!
   Astounding fact, with God we are one spirit,
     And differ not in life in any way!

Composition for prophecy with main point and sub-points: _____

_____

_____

_____

_____

_____

_____

_____

_____

_____

_____

_____

_____

_____

_____

_____

_____

_____

_____

_____

_____

_____

_____

_____

_____

_____

_____

_____

_____

_____

_____

_____

_____

_____

_____

_____

_____

Christ's Ministry in the Stage of Intensification to Produce the Overcomers

Scripture Reading: Rev. 1:10; 2:7; 4:5; 5:6; 17:14; 19:7; 21:10-11; 22:17a

Day 1 & Day 2

I. **There are three stages of Christ's ministry, and the work of the ministry to build up the Body of Christ is a threefold work (Eph. 4:11-12):**

A. The stage of incarnation is the stage of Christ in the flesh; the work in this stage produces redeemed people (John 1:14, 29; Rom. 3:24-25).

B. The stage of inclusion is the stage of Christ as the all-inclusive life-giving Spirit; the work in this stage produced the church and produces the churches (1 Cor. 15:45b; John 20:22; Phil. 1:19; Exo. 30:22-30; Heb. 2:12; Acts 8:1; 13:1; 14:23; 20:28).

C. The stage of intensification is the stage of Christ as the sevenfold intensified life-giving Spirit; the work in this stage produces the overcomers to deal with the degradation of the church and to produce the Body of Christ to consummate the New Jerusalem (Rev. 1:4; 3:1; 4:5; 5:6; 2:7, 17; 3:12, 20).

D. We need to carry out the threefold work of the ministry to produce redeemed ones, to establish churches, and to build up the Body consummating the New Jerusalem; the foundation is the work in the stage of incarnation, the building up is the work in the stage of inclusion, and the completion of the building is the work in the stage of intensification.

Day 3

II. **Christ's heavenly ministry is carried out in the divine and mystical realm of the consummated, life-giving, sevenfold intensified Spirit; in His heavenly ministry in the stage of intensification, He saves us from the degradation**

of the church (2 Tim. 1:15; 2:17-18; 4:10, 14-16; 2 Pet. 2:1, 15; 3:3-4, 15-16; 1 John 2:18, 22; 4:1-2, 6; 2 John 7, 9-11; 3 John 9-10):

A. He saves the believers in the church in Ephesus from the formal church life, which has lost the first love to the Lord, the shining capacity of the lampstand, and the enjoyment of Christ as life, to become overcomers so that they will be rewarded to eat of the tree of life in the Paradise of God—the New Jerusalem in the kingdom age (Rev. 2:1-7).

B. He strengthens the suffering believers in the church in Smyrna to overcome the persecution by being martyred so that they will be rewarded not to be hurt of the second death during the kingdom age (vv. 8-11).

C. He sanctifies the believers in the church in Pergamos from the union with the world and from the teachings of Balaam and the Nicolaitans to be the overcomers so that they may be rewarded to eat the hidden manna and to have a white stone upon which a new name will be written in the kingdom age (vv. 12-17).

D. He rescues the believers in the church in Thyatira from idol worship, fornication, demonic teachings, and the deep things of Satan to be the overcomers so that they may be rewarded with the authority over the nations in the kingdom age (vv. 18-29).

E. He revives the believers in the church in Sardis from their dead and dying condition to be the overcomers so that they may be rewarded with walking with the Lord in white and with not having their names erased out of the book of life but confessed by the Lord before the Father and His angels in the kingdom age (3:1-6).

F. He encourages the believers in the church in Philadelphia to hold fast what they have that no one take their crown to be the overcomers so that they may be rewarded to be a pillar in the temple of God and to have the name of God and the name of the New Jerusalem and the new name of the Lord written upon them in the kingdom age (vv. 7-13).

G. He awakens the believers in the church in Laodicea from their lukewarm and Christless condition, exhorting them to pay the price for the refined gold, white garments, and eyesalve and to open their door to the knocking Lord to be the overcomers to sit on the throne of the Lord in the kingdom age (vv. 14-22).

Day 4 III. **Christ saves us from the degradation of the church through His sevenfold intensified heavenly ministry by His up-to-date speaking and by our living in our spirit all the time:**

A. The speaking of the unlimited, life-releasing, sevenfold intensified, pneumatic Christ to the seven churches at the beginning of each epistle respectively becomes the speaking of the sevenfold intensified, all-inclusive life-giving Spirit to all the churches at the end of each epistle universally (2:1, 7-8, 11-12, 17-18, 29; 3:1, 6-7, 13-14, 22).

B. The overcoming of the church's degradation is by the participation of the overcoming saints who are living in their spirit (1:10; 4:2; 17:3; 21:10).

Day 5
&
Day 6 IV. **By Christ's sevenfold intensified heavenly ministry, He prepares His bride for His wedding and forms His bridal army to defeat and destroy His top enemies in humanity, the Antichrist and the false prophet (19:7-9, 11-21; 17:14):**

A. The overcomers, who are prepared to be Christ's bride, are raptured before the great tribulation for the purpose of defeating the enemy and satisfying God; God has a need for us to be raptured

so that we can be the firstfruits for His satisfaction and the man-child to fight against His
enemy (12:5, 7-11; 14:1, 4b; 19:7):

1. The meaning of rapture is to be taken into
   the Lord's presence; in order to be taken
   into the Lord's presence, we must be in His
   presence today and learn to have nearness
   and dearness in our contact with the Lord,
   having a heart that loves and treasures the
   Lord for His purpose (2 Cor. 2:10; 4:6-7).

2. Rapture is not mainly for our enjoyment
   but for God's enjoyment; we need to make
   ourselves ready to be raptured, not for our
   happiness but for the fulfillment of God's
   purpose (Rev. 19:7).

3. The rapture of the saints is the consummating step of God's organic salvation through
   Christ's sevenfold intensified heavenly ministry; by His sevenfold intensified organic
   salvation, we and the Lord become the same
   in appearance and expression (4:3; 21:11).

B. The final outcome of Christ's sevenfold intensified heavenly ministry is that the Bridegroom,
   as the consummated Spirit, and the bride, as the
   aggregate of all the overcomers, are united,
   mingled, and incorporated together to be one
   great God-man unto the praise of the glory of
   God's grace, with which He graced us in the
   Beloved (Eph. 1:6; Rev. 22:17a, 21).

Morning Nourishment

John ...The Word was God....And the Word became flesh
1:1, 14 and tabernacled among us...
20:22 And when He had said this, He breathed into *them* and said to them, Receive the Holy Spirit.
Rev. ...Grace to you and peace from Him who is and who
1:4-5 was and who is coming, and from the seven Spirits who are before His throne, and from Jesus Christ...

[Now] we will begin to consider the three stages of Christ, that is, the three periods of the history of what Christ is—incarnation, inclusion, and intensification. Many believers in Christ know something about the first stage of Christ's history, the stage of incarnation, but they know very little, if anything, about the second and third stages, the stages of inclusion and intensification.

Christians have paid a great deal of attention to the matter of incarnation, [but few realize its intrinsic significance]....Through incarnation Christ as God became flesh. John 1:14 tells us that the Word, who is the very God, became flesh.

In His resurrection the Christ who had become flesh through incarnation became the life-giving Spirit (1 Cor. 15:45b). Christ, therefore, has had two becomings. The first becoming is seen in John 1:14—the Word became flesh. The second becoming is seen in 1 Corinthians 15:45b—the last Adam (Christ in the flesh) became the life-giving Spirit....Christ's second becoming in resurrection is no less important than His first becoming in incarnation....Christ's becoming the life-giving Spirit in resurrection... involves something that we may designate by the word *inclusion*. (*Incarnation, Inclusion, and Intensification*, pp. 7-8)

Today's Reading

Christ's becoming flesh through incarnation was rather simple, for it involved just two parties—the Holy Spirit and a human virgin (Luke 1:26-27, 30-32, 35). Christ's becoming the life-giving Spirit, on the contrary, was not simple, for it involved and included divinity, humanity, Christ's death with its effectiveness, and Christ's resurrection with its power. In and through Christ's resurrection six things were compounded together to become the life-giving Spirit, which is God's anointing ointment (1 John 2:20, 27).

In Exodus 30 is the compound ointment as a type of the compound life-giving Spirit. The actual compounding of the Spirit took place in Christ's resurrection. It was in resurrection that the very God embodied in Christ and mingled with His humanity was compounded with Christ's death, the effectiveness of Christ's death, Christ's resurrection, and the power of His resurrection to produce the compound Spirit. This compounding was a matter of inclusion, for in the compound life-giving Spirit six items are included. Hence, the life-giving Spirit may be called the all-inclusive Spirit, the Spirit who includes divinity, humanity, the death of Christ and its effectiveness, and the resurrection of Christ and its power.

Whereas the incarnation was an objective matter, this inclusion is subjective to us and applicable to us in our experience....In the evening of the day of His resurrection, the Lord Jesus came as the compound Spirit and breathed into the disciples, saying, "Receive the Holy Spirit" [John 20:22]....As a part of the Body, those disciples represented the Body in receiving the inclusion, in receiving the compound Spirit. Because we can experience Christ in the stage of inclusion in such a subjective way, in this stage He is more applicable to us than He was in the stage of incarnation.

Not too long after the church was formed, it became degraded. The church should issue in the Body of Christ, but regrettably, as the Epistles reveal, the church gradually became degraded, even at Paul's time. Because of this degradation, the compound life-giving Spirit was intensified sevenfold to become the sevenfold intensified Spirit (Rev. 1:4; 5:6). This sevenfold intensified Spirit is for the overcoming of the degradation of the church and the producing of the overcomers so that the Body of Christ can be built up in a practical way to consummate the New Jerusalem, which is the unique and eternal goal of God's heart's desire. (*Incarnation, Inclusion, and Intensification,* pp. 8, 10-11)

Further Reading: Incarnation, Inclusion, and Intensification, ch. 1

Enlightenment and inspiration: _____

_____

_____

_____

Morning Nourishment

Rev.   ...And *there were* seven lamps of fire burning before
4:5   the throne, which are the seven Spirits of God.
5:6   And I saw in the midst of the throne...a Lamb stand-
       ing as having *just* been slain, having seven horns
       and seven eyes, which are the seven Spirits of God
       sent forth into all the earth.

In the first stage, the stage of Christ in the flesh, Christ produced a group of redeemed persons....Although a redeemed people had been produced, the church had not yet been produced.
The church was produced by Christ in the second stage. In this
stage Christ is the pneumatic Christ, the compound life-giving
Spirit, who produced the church on the day of Pentecost. The
redeemed saints, who were produced by Christ in the flesh,
became the church produced by Christ as the life-giving Spirit.

Shortly after the church was produced, it began to become
degraded....Eventually [it] degraded to such an extent that the Lord
could no longer tolerate it, and He reacted by intensifying Himself
sevenfold to become the sevenfold intensified Spirit (Rev. 1:4; 5:6).
He became intensified sevenfold to deal with the degradation of
the church. (*Incarnation, Inclusion, and Intensification,* p. 18)

Today's Reading

In his Epistles Paul spoke about the Body,...but I do not believe
that Paul saw the actual building up of the Body. Paul could see
the church expressed in various localities, but he could not see, in
actuality, the church as the Body in a perfect and complete way. In
order for the Body to be produced in a full and complete way, there
is the need of the third stage of Christ, the stage of intensification
in which Christ becomes the sevenfold intensified Spirit.

[In the book of Revelation we see that] Christ, who became the
compound, all-inclusive, life-giving Spirit, has become the sevenfold intensified Spirit. In Revelation 1:4 the third of the Divine
Trinity, the Spirit, becomes the seven Spirits and is [listed second].

The issue of Christ in the flesh was a group of redeemed persons, and the issue of Christ as the compound, all-inclusive, life-

giving Spirit was the churches. For the Body to be produced there is the need for the compound, all-inclusive, life-giving Spirit to be intensified sevenfold. This sevenfold intensification deals with the sevenfold situation of the seven churches in Revelation 2 and 3.

I am burdened that all the co-workers in the Lord's recovery would realize that we need to do a work of three sections. We should not only be able to do the work of the first section, the section of incarnation, to produce redeemed people, but we should also be able to do a work that can serve the purpose of the second section, the section of inclusion, to produce churches. Furthermore, we should be able to do a work to build up the Body of Christ consummating the New Jerusalem. This is the work of the stage of intensification.

The first stage—incarnation—is in the physical realm for the accomplishment of judicial redemption, which is a physical matter. The second stage—inclusion—is divine and mystical. In the third stage—intensification—there will be a maturing and a ripening in the divine and mystical realm, and the Body will be built up to consummate the New Jerusalem.

I hope that all the co-workers will see the three stages, the three sections, of Christ: incarnation—the stage of Christ in the flesh; inclusion—the stage of Christ as the life-giving Spirit; and intensification—the stage of Christ as the sevenfold intensified life-giving Spirit....Christ's history is divided into the section of His incarnation, the section of His inclusion, and the section of His intensification. Therefore we emphasize these three words—*incarnation, inclusion,* and *intensification*—and stress the facts that incarnation produces redeemed people, that inclusion produces the churches, and that intensification produces the overcomers to build up the Body, which consummates in the New Jerusalem as the unique goal of God's economy. This is the revelation in the New Testament. (*Incarnation, Inclusion, and Intensification,* pp. 19-21)

Further Reading: Incarnation, Inclusion, and Intensification, ch. 2

Enlightenment and inspiration: _____

_____

_____

_____

Morning Nourishment

Rev. To the messenger of the church in Ephesus write:...I
2:1-2, 4 know your works and your labor and your endurance....But I have *one thing* against you, that you
have left your first love.

3:1 And to the messenger of the church in Sardis write:
These things says He who has the seven Spirits of
God and the seven stars: I know your works, that you
have a name that you are living, and yet you are dead.

The first section of Christ's earthly ministry was accomplished
by Him judicially in the physical realm as the Christ in the flesh
from His incarnation to His death within His human age of
thirty-three and a half years.

The second section of His heavenly ministry is carried out by
Him organically in the mystical realm as the Christ as the life-
giving Spirit from His resurrection to the end of the millennium
within the age of the church and the age of the kingdom.

The third section of His sevenfold intensified heavenly ministry
is carried out by Him sevenfold intensified organically in the mystical realm as the Christ as the sevenfold intensified life-giving
Spirit from the degradation of the church to the coming of the new
heaven and new earth. (*The Divine and Mystical Realm*, pp. 71-72)

Today's Reading

The book of Revelation gives us a full record of the move of the
sevenfold Spirit in Christ's heavenly ministry....The sevenfold
intensified Spirit worked to save the believers in the church in
Ephesus from the formal church life, which had lost the first love
to the Lord, the shining capacity of the lampstand, and the enjoyment of Christ as life, to become overcomers so that they would be
rewarded to eat of the tree of life in the Paradise of God—the New
Jerusalem in the kingdom age (Rev. 2:1-7).

Christ as the sevenfold intensified life-giving Spirit worked to
strengthen the suffering believers...in Smyrna to overcome the
persecution by being martyred so that they would be rewarded
not to taste the second death during the kingdom age (2:8-11).

The church in Pergamos had become married to the world, so Christ as the sevenfold intensified life-giving Spirit worked to sanctify the believers there from the union with the world and from the teachings of Balaam and the Nicolaitans to be the overcomers so that they might be rewarded to eat the hidden manna and to have a white stone upon which a new name would be written in the kingdom age (2:12-17).

The sevenfold intensified life-giving Spirit works to rescue the believers in the church in Thyatira from idol worship, fornication, demonic teachings, and the deep things of Satan to be the overcomers so that they may be rewarded with the authority over the nations in the kingdom age (2:18-29).

Christ's sevenfold intensified heavenly ministry is to revive the believers in the church in Sardis from their dead and dying condition to be the overcomers so that they may be rewarded with walking with the Lord in white and with not having their names erased from the book of life but confessed by the Lord before the Father and His angels in the kingdom age (3:1-6).

Although Philadelphia is the best church, the believers there need to hold fast what they have that no one take their crown to be the overcomers so that they may be rewarded to be a pillar in the temple of God with the name of God and the name of the New Jerusalem and the new name of the Lord written upon them in the kingdom age (3:7-13). The name which is upon them indicates that this is what they are. That means that they are the New Jerusalem,...God,...[and] the Lord Jesus....Of course, their being God and the Lord Jesus is in life and in nature but not in the Godhead.

The believers in the church in Laodicea need to be awakened from their lukewarm and Christless condition. Thus, the Lord exhorts them to pay the price for the refined gold, white garments, and eyesalve and to open their door to the knocking Lord to be the overcomers so that they may be rewarded to sit on the throne of the Lord in the kingdom age (3:14-22). (*The Divine and Mystical Realm*, pp. 72-74)

Further Reading: The Divine and Mystical Realm, ch. 5

Enlightenment and inspiration: _____

_____

_____

_____

Morning Nourishment

Rev. And I saw...a Lamb standing as having *just* been
5:6 slain, having seven horns and seven eyes, which are
     the seven Spirits of God sent forth into all the earth.
2:1 To the messenger of the church in Ephesus write:
     These things says He who holds the seven stars in
     His right hand, He who walks in the midst of the
     seven golden lampstands.
2:7 He who has an ear, let him hear what the Spirit says
     to the churches. To him who overcomes, to him I will
     give to eat of the tree of life, which is in the Paradise
     of God.

We are saved from degradation by the speaking of the unlimited, life-releasing, sevenfold intensified pneumatic Christ (the Lamb with the seven Spirits as His eyes—Rev. 5:6). The seven Spirits are the eyes of Christ, who is the Lamb. No one can separate your eyes from your person. The sevenfold Spirit being the eyes of Christ indicates that they are one with Christ. The speaking of the sevenfold intensified pneumatic Christ to the seven churches at the beginning of each epistle respectively becomes the speaking of the sevenfold intensified, all-inclusive, life-giving Spirit to all the seven churches at the end of each epistle universally (Rev. 2:1, 7;...3:1, 6,...14, 22). At the beginning of each epistle Christ is speaking, and at the end the Spirit is speaking. This shows that Christ is the Spirit. (*The Divine and Mystical Realm,* pp. 74-75)

Today's Reading

The overcoming of the degradation is by the participation of the overcoming saints who are living in their spirit (Rev. 1:10; 4:2; 17:3; 21:10). On the one hand, our overcoming is by Christ's speaking becoming the Spirit's speaking. On the other hand, it is by our living in our spirit all the time. In Revelation 1:10 John said that on the Lord's Day he was in spirit. This shows that John the apostle was a man in the spirit, always living in the spirit.

Christ's sevenfold intensified heavenly ministry is for the complete preparation of the bride for Christ the Bridegroom to have His triumphant wedding in the millennium for His satisfaction according to His good pleasure (Rev. 19:7-9).

Christ's sevenfold intensified heavenly ministry is also for the formation of the bridal army for Christ to defeat and destroy His top enemies in humanity, the Antichrist and his false prophet (Rev. 19:11-21; 17:14). The coming Antichrist and his false prophet will be human enemies of Christ,...but Christ and His bride will destroy them and throw them into the lake of fire.

Christ's sevenfold intensified heavenly ministry is for the binding of Satan and the casting of him into the abyss for one thousand years (Rev. 20:1-3).

His sevenfold intensified heavenly ministry is also for the bringing in of the kingdom of Christ and of God, which will be the millennium (Rev. 20:4-6).

Ultimately, Christ's sevenfold intensified heavenly ministry is for the initial consummation of the New Jerusalem in the millennium (Rev. 2:7) and its full consummation in the new heaven and new earth (21:2). In other words, the New Jerusalem will be consummated by the overcomers first in the initial part in the thousand years on a small scale and then in eternity on a full scale. All the believers, through the discipline of the one thousand years, will be matured, transformed, and conformed, to participate in the New Jerusalem in eternity.

The final outcome is that the ultimately consummated Spirit as the consummation of the processed Triune God becomes the Bridegroom and the aggregate of the overcoming saints becomes the bride of the universal romance between the redeeming God and His redeemed man as the conclusion of the entire Scriptures (Rev. 22:17)....The Bridegroom is God as the consummated Spirit, and the bride is the aggregate of all the overcomers. This is all accomplished by the additional section of the sevenfold intensified organic salvation of God. (*The Divine and Mystical Realm*, pp. 75-76)

Further Reading: The Secret of God's Organic Salvation—"The Spirit Himself with Our Spirit," ch. 6

Enlightenment and inspiration: _____

_____

_____

_____

Morning Nourishment

Rev.   And she brought forth a son, a man-child, who is to
12:5   shepherd all the nations with an iron rod; and her
       child was caught up to God and to His throne.
14:4   ...These were purchased from among men *as* first-
       fruits to God and to the Lamb.

You may be wondering about the difference between the
overcomers in Revelation 12 and the overcomers in chapter fourteen. In chapter twelve we have the man-child, and in chapter
fourteen we have the firstfruits....The man-child is for fighting
and defeating Satan. Hence, the man-child deals with the enemy.
The firstfruits are not for fighting; they are for the satisfaction of
God and the Lamb. God and the Lamb need enjoyment. We, the
living overcomers, shall be the firstfruits to satisfy Their need for
enjoyment.

The enemy, the devil, in heaven must be cast down by the
man-child, who will execute the Lord's judgment over him. This is
the function of the man-child. But there is another need in the
heavens—God must be satisfied. God is hungry and thirsty. He
desires some firstfruits to taste for His satisfaction. (*Life-study of
Revelation*, p. 536)

Today's Reading

Here again we see the sovereign wisdom of the Lord. The
overcomers who have died throughout the centuries will be the
man-child, the fighters. Although we who are living on earth
must also fight against the enemy, there is no need to fight him all
the time. After you have preached to Satan for a while, you should
forget about him. The enemy is subtle. Once you begin to preach
to him, he will attract you to preach to him constantly...in order
to distract you from loving the Lord. Therefore, after preaching to
the devil for a period of time, you should say, "Devil, I have no
more time to preach to you. Rather, I would use my time to tell my
Lord how much I love Him. I want to remain with my Lord in a
loving way. Satan, you are the Lord's enemy and you are my
enemy too. I have preached enough to you. Get away—now is the

time for me to enjoy a honeymoon with my Lord." Learn this strategy....Learn to spend time loving the Lord Jesus in an intimate way. If you have never had such a time, you are short. It is not adequate merely to be sinless. It is not sufficient simply to be good or right. We must be in love with the Lord. Although I do not like the term *in love,* I am forced to use it. We all need to fall in love with the Lord Jesus, telling Him, "O Lord Jesus, I love You, and You know that I love You. Because I love You, Lord, there are certain things that I will not do." This is the way to be a living overcomer. Although the Lord certainly needs the man-child to fight against His enemy, He needs the firstfruits, His lovers, even more to be His satisfaction.

In type, the firstfruits were brought not to the farmer's home, but into God's house, the temple, for His satisfaction. This was even true of the Lord Jesus as the firstfruits (1 Cor. 15:20, 23). On the morning of His resurrection, the Lord did not allow Mary to touch Him. He said, "Do not touch Me, for I have not yet ascended to the Father" (John 20:17). The Lord seemed to be saying, "Do not touch Me, because I must present My freshness in My resurrection to My Father. My Father must be the first to taste the freshness of My resurrection." We all need to learn to present ourselves in a fresh, intimate, and loving way to the Lord for His enjoyment. If you decline to do...or to touch certain things simply because you are afraid,...you are not on the high plane of being a lover of the Lord. Rather, you are down on the lowest level. We must be on the highest plane, refusing to do certain things, not out of fear, but out of love for the Lord. The sisters desire to be with their husbands instead of going home to their parents because they love their husbands. Likewise, because I love the Lord, I shall refrain from doing certain things. I may have the liberty to do them, and it may not be wrong to do them, but simply because of my love for the Lord Jesus, I would not do them. This is the true significance of this portion of the Word. (*Life-study of Revelation,* pp. 536-538)

Further Reading: Life-study of Revelation, msg. 46

Enlightenment and inspiration: _____

_____

_____

_____

Morning Nourishment

Exo. The first of the firstfruits of your ground you shall
23:19 bring into the house of Jehovah your God.
Rev. These are they who have not been defiled with
14:4-5 women, for they are virgins. These are they who
follow the Lamb wherever He may go. These were
purchased from among men *as* firstfruits to God and
to the Lamb. And in their mouth no lie was found;
they are without blemish.
22:17 And the Spirit and the bride say, Come!...

We need to follow the principle in Revelation 14:4. This principle is that we, sisters and brothers alike, must keep our virginity,
looking to the Lord that, by His grace, He would preserve us for
Himself. We should be not only fighters but also firstfruits, those
who ripen earlier for the Lord's satisfaction. We need to say, "Lord,
for the sake of Your satisfaction, I want to ripen early. Lord, I don't
care for my rapture—I care for Your satisfaction. I want to be
taken to the heavens to satisfy You. Lord, as long as I can satisfy
You, it makes no difference to me whether I am on earth or in
heaven." This is the attitude of the living overcomers.

Because it does not matter to the firstfruits where they are, we
are not told that they are caught up; instead, we are simply told
that the one hundred forty-four thousand firstfruits are standing
with the Lamb on Mount Zion....This surely is not the Zion on
earth, but the Zion in the heavens. If you are one of the living
overcomers, it will make no difference to you whether or not you
are raptured. Because you are already in the Lord's presence, the
rapture will not come as a surprise. It does not matter to you
whether you are in His presence here on earth or there on Mount
Zion....Are you truly loving the Lord? Are you in intimate fellowship with Him right now, being kept in Him as a virgin? If you are,
then the rapture will not come as a surprise; it will be an ordinary
experience. (*Life-study of Revelation,* pp. 538-539)

Today's Reading

Although these verses on the firstfruits point to one kind of rapture, they actually say nothing about rapture. We are told that the man-child is "caught-up," but we are told that the firstfruits are standing on Mount Zion with the Lamb. If you were to ask them when they got there, they might say, "We are simply here. We have no special feeling about being here because we have been in the Lord's presence for years. We have lived in this atmosphere for a long time." This is the rapture of the living overcomers. These are the firstfruits, those who satisfy the hunger of God the Father and the Lamb, the Redeemer. The earliest ones of God's crop to mature are not for fighting; they are for satisfaction.

Revelation 14:5 says,…"In their mouth no lie was found." Lies are the expression and representation of Satan. The devil is the father of all liars, and lies come out of him (John 8:44). That no lie was found in the overcomers' mouth indicates that there is nothing of Satan in their expression. If we live a life of loving the Lord, then no lie or falsehood will proceed out of our mouth. Although I hate to say it, for years I have suffered the lies of genuine Christians. What a shame! In the Lord's recovery there should be no lies and no falsehood in our mouth. When we say "Yes," we mean yes, and when we say "No," we mean no. If we cannot answer with a clear yes or no, we should not say anything. In such a case we should exercise our wisdom to say nothing, so that no lies nor falsehood would come out of our mouth. We have nothing to do with Satan, the liar and the source of the lies.

Revelation 14:5 also says that the firstfruits are without blemish. This indicates that they are without spot or wrinkle, but are perfect in the holiness of God (Eph. 5:27), absolutely sanctified to God and fully saturated with God (1 Thes. 5:23).

The one hundred forty-four thousand firstfruits "follow the Lamb wherever He may go" (v. 4). It is not that the Lamb follows us, but that we follow Him wherever He goes. We all must learn the lesson of following Him wherever He goes. (*Life-study of Revelation,* pp. 539-540)

Further Reading: Life-study of Revelation, msg. 46

Enlightenment and inspiration: _____

_____

_____

_____

Hymns, #1314

1   Lord, Thou wilt soon appear,
      Thy day is almost here.
  Oh, how we love Thy coming soon!
    We have no other
    Lord, life, or lover
  Than Thou, Lord Jesus, our Bridegroom!

2   The hour is drawing nigh,
      Soon we shall hear Thy cry
  And see Thee in the clouds descend.
    Oh what an hour sweet
    When Bride and Bridegroom meet
  And love surpassing comprehend.

3   The moments fly apace,
      Soon we shall see Thy face!
  Amen, Lord Jesus! Quickly come!
    We long Thyself to see
    And with Thee ever be,
  Thou who our inmost heart hath won.

4   'Tis but a moment now;
      Thou, our Lord Bridegroom, Thou
  Soon wilt return to claim Thy Bride.
    O Hallelujah!
    'Tis this we long for,
  And Thou too wilt be satisfied.

Composition for prophecy with main point and sub-points: _____

_____

_____

_____

_____

_____

_____

_____

_____

_____

_____

_____

_____

_____

_____

_____

_____

_____

_____

_____

_____

_____

_____

_____

_____

_____

_____

_____

_____

_____

_____

_____

_____

_____

The Vision of the Woman, the Dragon, and the Man-child

Scripture Reading: Rev. 12:1-17; 11:15

Day 1 I. **Among the many crucial matters in the second section of the book of Revelation, the first is the vision of the universal bright woman with her man-child warring against the great red dragon (Rev. 12:1-17):**
   A. The vision in Revelation 12 covers all the generations from Genesis 3:15 until the end of this age (Rev. 11:15; 12:10).
   B. Revelation 12 gives us a view of what is taking place in the universe; here we see that God's enemy is fighting against Him (v. 17).
   C. This vision of the true situation in the universe must become a governing vision to us (Prov. 29:18a; Acts 26:19):
      1. If we see this vision, our concept regarding the Christian life will be radically changed (2 Cor. 5:9-10).
      2. Seeing this controlling vision will help us to be in the genuine oneness and to bring forth the man-child to defeat God's enemy and bring in God's kingdom (John 17:11, 21-24; Rev. 12:5, 10; 11:15).

Day 2 II. **"A great sign was seen in heaven: a woman clothed with the sun, and the moon underneath her feet, and on her head a crown of twelve stars; and she was with child" (12:1-2a):**
   A. This bright woman is a collective, universal woman signifying the totality of God's people (v. 1).
   B. God's intention is, through the universal woman, to bring forth the man-child—the stronger part of God's people—whom He will use to defeat His enemy and bring in His kingdom (vv. 10-11).

C. Throughout all generations God's people have been suffering the travail of delivery to bring forth the man-child to fight for God's kingdom (Isa. 26:17-18; Jer. 6:24; 13:21; 30:6; Micah 4:9-10; 5:3; Gal. 4:19).

Day 3
D. For the bringing forth of the man-child, there is the need for at least a portion of God's people to come back to the proper standing of the woman and become part of the woman in an actual and practical way (2 Cor. 11:2; Eph. 5:24).

E. The woman in Revelation 12 is submissive to her Husband and has been impregnated by her Husband in order to bring forth something for her Husband (vv. 2, 5):
  1. The church's duty is not mainly to do something for Christ but to receive something of Christ so that she may be made pregnant of Christ and may bring forth the man-child for Christ (Gal. 1:15-16; 2:20; 4:19; Phil. 1:21).
  2. We need to be constantly open to the Lord as our Husband to permit the element of Christ, the divine constituent of Christ, to work in us continually to saturate and permeate our whole being (Matt. 5:3; Gal. 4:19; Eph. 3:16-17a).

Day 4
III. "Another sign was seen in heaven; and behold, there was a great red dragon...The dragon stood before the woman who was about to bring forth, so that when she brings forth he might devour her child" (Rev. 12:3a, 4b):
A. The dragon signifies God's enemy, called the Devil and Satan; the serpent is the subtle one, and the dragon is the cruel one (v. 9; Gen. 3:1; 2 Cor. 11:3).
B. We need to see the vision that in the universe a war is raging between God's people as the woman and the serpent as the dragon (Gen. 3:15; Rev. 12:17):

1. The enmity between the serpent and the woman's seed mentioned in Genesis 3:15 is manifested in Revelation 12, where this enmity is fulfilled to the uttermost.

2. The dragon hates the universal bright woman, and he fights against her with the intention of devouring her child (vv. 4, 13-17).

Day 5   **IV. "She brought forth a son, a man-child, who is to shepherd all the nations with an iron rod" (v. 5a):**

A. God needs the man-child to defeat His enemy and to bring in His kingdom so that His eternal purpose might be accomplished (v. 10; Eph. 3:11; 2 Tim. 1:9).

B. Because the church has not attained to God's purpose, God will choose a group of overcomers who will attain to His purpose and fulfill His demands; this is the principle of the man-child (Rev. 12:11; 2:7, 11, 17, 26-28; 3:5, 12, 20-21).

C. The stronger ones among God's people are a collective unit fighting the battle for God and bringing God's kingdom down to earth (Eph. 6:10-11; Rev. 12:10).

D. The woman's seed in Revelation 12 is not only the individual Christ but is a corporate entity, the corporate Christ, including Christ as the Head and all His overcoming believers as the Body (Col. 1:18):

1. The man-child is not individual but corporate; the man-child is neither the Lord Jesus individually nor the overcomers separate from Him but the Lord Jesus with the overcomers (Psa. 2:9; Rev. 2:27; 12:5).

2. The Lord Jesus is the Head, the center, the reality, the life, and the nature of the man-child, and the overcomers are the Body of the man-child.

Day 6   E. The entire being of the man-child is saturated and permeated with the element of Christ; the

way to become the man-child is to be strengthened into our inner man so that Christ may
build Himself into our hearts, to be nourished
with the unsearchable riches of Christ, and to
put on Christ as the whole armor of God (Eph.
3:16-18, 8; 6:10-11; Gal. 4:19).

V. "The kingdom of the world has become the
kingdom of our Lord and of His Christ, and
He will reign forever and ever" (Rev. 11:15):

A. The man-child is related to God's most important dispensational move—His move to end this
age and bring in the age of the kingdom (12:10;
Matt. 6:9-10).

B. God wants to end this age and bring in the age
of the kingdom, and for this He must have the
man-child as His dispensational instrument
(13:43a).

C. The rapture of the man-child to heaven, the
casting of Satan to earth, and the declaration
in heaven signify that the man-child will bring
the kingdom to earth; this is God's greatest
dispensational move (Rev. 12:5, 9-10; 11:15).

Morning Nourishment

Gen.   And I will put enmity between you and the woman
3:15   and between your seed and her seed; he will bruise
        you on the head, but you will bruise him on the heel.
Rev.   And the great dragon was cast down, the ancient
12:9-10 serpent, he who is called the Devil and Satan, he who
        deceives the whole inhabited earth; he was cast to
        the earth....And I heard a loud voice in heaven saying,
        Now has come the salvation and the power and the
        kingdom of our God and the authority of His Christ,
        for the accuser of our brothers has been cast down,
        who accuses them before our God day and night.

[In Revelation 12] we see a bright woman representing God
and a dragon signifying God's enemy. We also see that these two
are fighting. Praise the Lord that we are not only part of the
woman, but we are also becoming part of the man-child, the
stronger part of the woman that fights against the dragon. We are
fighting the dragon today, and one day we shall be there in the
heavens to give him the word to leave heaven....Among the many
crucial matters in the second section of the book of Revelation the
first is this vision of the universal bright woman with her man-
child warring against the dragon. This must be a governing
vision. As long as we see it, we shall know where we are, what we
must do, and where we shall be. We are in the church, we must be
in the man-child, and our destiny is to be raptured to heaven that
we may issue the order to Michael to cast Satan and his angels
out of heaven. If we see this vision, we shall surely be beside ourselves. (*Life-study of Revelation,* pp. 457-458)

Today's Reading

There are three main figures in Revelation 12: the woman, the
man-child, and the great red dragon. Throughout the centuries,
there has been war between the woman and the serpent. Actually, the battle has not been fought by the woman, but by the man-
child. This chapter covers all the generations from Genesis 3:15
until the end of this age.

The principle in becoming the firstfruits or the man-child is the same: we must follow the Lamb wherever He goes (Rev. 14:4). However,...following the Lamb is not an outward matter....If the element of the Lamb does not get into us, we shall be unable to follow Him....To follow the Lamb means to allow the Lamb to get into you. When the element of the Lamb is constituted into your being, you will actually be a part of the Lamb. You will be unable to be what you were before because you have been transformed. Our transformed being is the man-child. Now we are the woman submitting to our husband and receiving something of Him into our being. If we allow the element that we have received of our husband to saturate and permeate our being, constituting us with this element, we shall no longer be simply the woman, but the man-child.

As individuals, you and I are not the woman. Only together, as a corporate unit, are we all the one woman. Since there is only one woman, whoever of God's people is dissenting is finished with this woman. The only way we can be one is to submit ourselves to Christ and to receive something of Christ. If we do not submit to Him, we cannot be one. True oneness only comes from submitting ourselves to our one Husband, to the unique headship. Furthermore, we must only receive the unique element of Christ. Although we may have different concepts, we should not receive anything of our concept. If you receive something of your concept, you will be divided immediately.

If you have seen the vision, you will never accept any concept, proposal, criticism, suggestion, or doubt. You will only receive something of Christ....If we submit ourselves to our one Husband and only receive something of Him,...we shall be one and shall bring forth the man-child to defeat God's enemy and to bring in God's kingdom. (*Life-study of Revelation,* pp. 435, 416, 418)

Further Reading: Life-study of Genesis, msg. 20; *A General Sketch of the New Testament in the Light of Christ and the Church, Part 4: Revelation,* ch. 38

Enlightenment and inspiration: _____

_____

_____

_____

Morning Nourishment

Rev. And a great sign was seen in heaven: a woman
12:1-2 clothed with the sun, and the moon underneath her
feet, and on her head a crown of twelve stars; and
she was with child, and she cried out, travailing in
birth and being in pain to bring forth.

Gal. My children, with whom I travail again in birth until
4:19 Christ is formed in you.

In Genesis 3:15 the woman was local and individual; the seed,
Christ, was also individual; and the serpent was a small snake.
All three, the woman, the seed, and the serpent, were individual
and on a small scale. But in Revelation 12 the woman is universal
and collective, symbolizing all of God's people: the patriarchs represented by the twelve stars; Israel represented by the moon; and
the church, the New Testament believers, represented by the sun.
In Revelation 12 the serpent has become a dragon. While the serpent creeps on earth, the dragon flies through the air. Now Satan
not only moves on the earth but is also exceedingly active in the
air. The seed in this chapter is not just the individual Christ but is
a corporate entity, the corporate Christ, including Christ as the
Head and all His overcoming believers as the Body. Hence, the
three items found in Genesis 3:15 are seen in a highly developed
form in Revelation 12. (*Life-study of Revelation*, p. 419)

Today's Reading

In Joseph's dream [Gen. 37:9], the sun, the moon, and the
eleven stars plus Joseph himself signified the total composition of
God's people on earth. Based upon the principle of that dream, the
sun, the moon, and the twelve stars here must signify the totality
of God's people on earth, which in this chapter is symbolized by a
woman.

Most of her being is clothed with the sun. The sun signifies
God's people in the New Testament age. Before Christ came into
the world, it was the dark night of the Old Testament age. When
Christ came, it was the rising sun visiting us from on high (Luke
1:78), the beginning of the age of the sun. Before that, it was the

age of the moon, which signifies God's people in the Old Testament time. The moon is under the feet of the woman, for the age of the moon was the age of the law, which should not be exalted as the stars. The stars, which signify the patriarchs, God's people before the law was given, are on her head as a crown. All God's people in these three ages, who together constitute this woman, are light bearers. Hence, she is the bright woman shining throughout all generations.

Before God's people can be the man-child, they must firstly be a woman to Him. This indicates that we in the church today must firstly be the woman to God and then the man-child. By the sign in Revelation 12 we see that God's intention is to bring forth a man-child through this woman. The woman has been and still is the means by which God can bring forth this man-child, the one whom God will use to defeat His enemy and to bring in His kingdom. In other words, God will use this man-child to fulfill His economy and to accomplish His purpose. This is a great matter. In order to accomplish His purpose, God not only needs the individual Christ but also a corporate Christ, the church, God's people. We do not agree with the concept that this woman is merely the mother of Jesus or the nation of Israel. She is the universal, corporate body of God's people. God needs the man-child to defeat His enemy and to bring in His kingdom that His eternal purpose might be accomplished. In order for Him to have such a man-child, there is the need of the woman.

The man-child is brought forth by the suffering woman, by the suffering people of God (vv. 2, 4-5). The words *cried out* in verse 2 signify that she was praying. "Travailing in birth and being in pain to bring forth" signifies that throughout all generations God's people have been suffering the travail of delivery (Isa. 26:17-18; Jer. 6:24; 13:21; 30:6; Micah 4:9-10; 5:3; Gal. 4:19) to bring forth the man-child to fight for God's kingdom. (*Life-study of Revelation,* pp. 402, 411-412, 432-433)

Further Reading: Life-study of Revelation, msgs. 34, 39

Enlightenment and inspiration: _____

_____
_____
_____

Morning Nourishment

2 Cor. For I am jealous over you with a jealousy of God; for
11:2   I betrothed you to one husband to present *you as* a
      pure virgin to Christ.

Eph. But as the church is subject to Christ, so also *let* the
5:24   wives *be subject* to their husbands in everything.

Phil. For to me, to live is Christ...
1:21

According to the Bible, in order for a woman to be a proper wife, she must submit to her husband. In this universe the unique husband, the unique man, is God. God...is our husband. Whether we are males or females by birth, being God's people, we are females in God's eyes. God is our husband, and we are His counterpart. As His wife, we must submit ourselves to Him.

A wife must also receive something from her husband in order to become pregnant. The Bible reveals that submission is to receive something of Christ, just as the woman submits to her husband, not to do something for him but to receive something of him. Nothing that a wife does for her husband is more important than receiving something of her husband. Actually a wife's duty is not to do things for her husband; it is to receive something of her husband that she may bring forth something for her husband. In the great sign in Revelation 12, the woman is not portrayed as doing anything for her husband; she is pictured as being pregnant. She has been impregnated by her husband in order to bring forth something for her husband. (*Life-study of Revelation*, pp. 412-413)

Today's Reading

The church's duty is not mainly to do something for Christ. Her duty is to receive something of Christ that she may be made pregnant of Christ and may bring forth something for Christ.

The woman in Revelation 12 firstly indicates submission to God. Secondly, she indicates that we do not need to do anything for God. What we need is to receive something of God. He does not need anything of us, but we need something of Christ to enter into our being that we might be made pregnant and might bring forth something for Him. The church today needs Christ. This vision is altogether lacking in today's Christianity....As the proper woman, we must firstly submit ourselves to our Husband, not to do something for Him, but to receive something of Him. If we do this we shall be made pregnant, and something will be brought forth through us.

Only by receiving Christ into our being can we bring forth the man-child. The man-child is formed wholly of the constituent of Christ. In order to produce the man-child, we must first be one with Christ and receive something of Him. When we receive something uniquely of Christ, we shall be made pregnant of Christ to bring forth the man-child. If you see this vision, you will feel sorrowful about the situation in today's Christianity.

We need to constantly be open to our Husband. We must permit the element of Christ, the divine constituent of Christ, to work in us continually to saturate and permeate our whole being. Today, the Lord's desire is that many of His children realize that, as God's people, we are His wife for the purpose of bringing forth the man-child. We cannot produce or manufacture this man-child; we must receive something of Christ and be made pregnant of Him. Something of our Christ must enter into our being. It is not a matter of our being humble, patient, nice, or good. It is absolutely a matter of opening our being to His divine element and of allowing this element to be worked into us. For this, we need "nine months." It takes this long for the man-child to be developed within us.

The apostle Paul said in Galatians 4:19, "I travail again in birth until Christ is formed in you." This indicates that he realized that he was part of this travailing woman to bring forth the man-child, which is Christ formed in us. Then in Philippians 1:21 he said, "For to me, to live is Christ." This indicates that he became a part of the man-child by experiencing Christ....Paul was set up by God as a pattern for the believers (1 Tim. 1:16). We all must be like him. (*Life-study of Revelation,* pp. 413-414, 416)

Further Reading: Life-study of Revelation, msg. 35; *The Glorious Church,* ch. 4

Enlightenment and inspiration: _____

_____

_____

_____

Morning Nourishment

Rev. **And another sign was seen in heaven; and behold,**
12:3-4 *there was* **a great red dragon, having seven heads and**
ten horns, and on his heads seven diadems....And the
dragon stood before the woman who was about to
bring forth, so that when she brings forth he might
devour her child.

11 **And they overcame him because of the blood of the**
Lamb and because of the word of their testimony, and
they loved not their soul-life even unto death.

On the one hand, we should be part of the woman to travail for
the birth of the man-child and, on the other hand, we should be
the man-child to defeat God's enemy and to bring in His kingdom
for the fulfilling of His purpose.

The enemy hates this woman and is seeking to devour the
man-child. The warfare is due to the enemy's desire to put this
woman out of function....Sometimes I wonder why people oppose
us so much....Humanly speaking, it is very difficult to understand this. Even many of the opposers and critics do not know the
reason. But the great dragon knows. He realizes that some of
God's people are resuming the true position of the woman. Once
we have resumed this position, God has the opportunity to bring
forth the man-child. Satan, the subtle one behind the opposers,
knows that some of God's people have taken the position of this
woman and that they will be made pregnant of Christ to bring
forth the man-child. In this warfare we must touch the throne,
call upon the highest authority, and exercise our spirit to fight the
battle. (*Life-study of Revelation*, p. 417)

Today's Reading

That the dragon stood before the woman [in Revelation 12:4]
signifies that Satan is always against the people of God. From the
time of Genesis 3:15 to this day, Satan has been continually fighting against the woman with the intention of devouring her child.
(*Life-study of Revelation*, p. 438)

The enmity between the serpent and the woman's seed

mentioned in Genesis 3:15 is fully manifested in Revelation 12,...[where] the old serpent tries his best to damage the man-child and the woman (vv. 4, 13-17). The enmity of Genesis 3:15 is thus fulfilled to the uttermost. (*Life-study of Genesis,* p. 254)

[Revelation 12:3 speaks of a "great red dragon."] How did the serpent in Genesis 3 become the dragon in Revelation 12? It was by eating a great deal. Through his eating, the serpent has been continually increasing. Many have been feeding him, and now he is trying to devour us. But we will never be devoured by him; rather, we will give him a death blow. When the Lord cursed the serpent, He assigned him to eat dust (Gen. 3:14). As long as we are dusty, earthy, we are food for the serpent. But if we are heav-enly, the serpent cannot devour us. We are not dusty or earthy; we are a part of the heavenly, bright woman.

We must see the vision that in the universe a warfare is raging between the woman and the dragon. Whoever persecutes the church is one with the dragon....In chapter seventeen, we see a beast with seven heads and ten horns, the same number of heads and horns that the dragon has (Rev. 12:3; 17:3). On this beast sits a woman clothed in purple and scarlet and gilded with gold and precious stone and pearls (17:3-4). The apostate Catholic Church, being the prostitute riding on the beast, is one with the dragon in persecuting the bright woman....The Pharisees, although they were Jews, were not a part of the moon. The Lord Jesus called them "serpents" and the "generation of vipers" (Matt. 23:33). They were "the seed of the serpent," as mentioned in Genesis 3:15.... They had become part of the great dragon.

Any Christians who persecute the church are one with the dragon, taking sides with him against God's economy. If we have this vision, we shall see that there can be no neutral ground. There are only two parties—the woman or the dragon. (*Life-study of Revelation,* pp. 406-408)

Further Reading: Life-study of Revelation, msg. 37; *Life-study of Genesis,* msg. 19

Enlightenment and inspiration: _____

_____

_____

_____

Morning Nourishment

Rev. And she brought forth a son, a man-child, who is to
12:5 shepherd all the nations with an iron rod; and her
child was caught up to God and to His throne.
Eph. Finally, be empowered in the Lord and in the might of
6:10-11 His strength. Put on the whole armor of God that you
may be able to stand against the stratagems of the devil.
2 Tim. Who has saved us and called us with a holy calling,
1:9 not according to our works but according to His own
purpose...

Firstly, the Lord's economy is with His people represented by
the woman. But the Lord's economy cannot be carried out merely
by the woman. There is the need of the strong ones. This is always
the principle. We must be absolute and strong. If we would take
this way, we would take it absolutely. But if we would not take it,
then we would forget about it. We must not only be part of the
woman, but also part of the man-child within the woman. It is not
adequate simply to be in the Lord's recovery. We have to be among
that part in the Lord's recovery which is strong. Whatever tests
and trials may come, we would stand against them.

We are here for the Lord's recovery and for nothing else.
Remember that the Lord's recovery is the practicality of His econ-
omy today. His economy can only be carried out by the man-child.
(*Life-study of Revelation,* pp. 422-423)

Today's Reading

The Scripture says that this man-child will "shepherd all the
nations with an iron rod" [Rev. 12:5]. This is God's purpose. The
work of the church is to cause Satan to lose his power and bring in
God's kingdom. The church which God desires must have the char-
acteristic...of cooperation with Christ. Since the church, however,
has not attained to God's purpose, nor does she even know God's
purpose,...[God] will choose a group of overcomers who will
attain His purpose and fulfill His demand. This is the principle of
the man-child. (Watchman Nee, *The Glorious Church,* p. 81)

Verse 2 says that the woman "was with child," and verse 5 says that "she brought forth a son, a man-child." The child here, being a man-child, signifies the stronger part of God's people. Although in verse 2 this child was in the woman, the Word does not call him a baby, but a man-child....The woman represents the totality of God's people. But throughout all generations there have been some stronger ones among God's people. These are considered in the Bible as a collective unit fighting the battle for God and bringing God's kingdom down to earth. (*Life-study of Revelation,* pp. 419-420)

Some say that the man-child is the Lord Jesus. I agree with this in a sense because the Lord Jesus is the Head, the center, the reality, the life, and the nature of the man-child. However, this man-child is not individual; he is corporate. Since the woman herself is not individual, but universal and corporate, her child must also be universal and corporate. This corporate man-child includes the Lord Jesus....This can be proved from the Scriptures. Psalm 2:8-9 prophesies that the Lord Jesus, God's anointed One, will rule the nations with a rod of iron. Revelation 2:26-27 says that the overcomers in the churches will rule over the nations with a rod of iron. Now in Revelation 12:5 we are told that the man-child will rule all nations with a rod of iron. Therefore,... both the Lord Jesus Himself and His overcomers will rule over the nations with a rod of iron. Thus, the man-child in Revelation 12:5 includes both the Lord Jesus and the overcomers in the churches. Furthermore, Revelation 20:4 says that Christ and the resurrected overcomers will reign as kings for a thousand years. Hence, the man-child in Revelation 12 is neither the Lord Jesus individually nor the overcomers separate from Him, but the Lord Jesus with the overcomers. Christ Himself is the foremost overcomer (Rev. 3:21). As the leading overcomer He is the Head, center, reality, life, and nature of the overcomers. Among the people of God on earth there is a stronger part which includes the Lord Jesus and the overcomers. Thus, the Lord Jesus and His overcomers compose the man-child. (*Life-study of Genesis,* pp. 253-254)

Further Reading: Life-study of Revelation, msgs. 36, 38

Enlightenment and inspiration: _____

_____

_____

_____

Morning Nourishment

Matt. You then pray in this way: Our Father who is in the
6:9-10 heavens, Your name be sanctified; Your kingdom
come; Your will be done, as in heaven, *so* also on earth.
Rev. ...There were loud voices in heaven, saying, The king-
11:15 dom of the world has become the *kingdom* of our Lord
and of His Christ, and He will reign forever and ever.

The man-child is the stronger part of the woman....We firstly
must be the woman;...we must also be the man-child. It is not
adequate simply to be bright and heavenly. We must be fully constituted with the element of Christ. The difference between the
woman and the man-child is this: not much of the element of
Christ is constituted into the being of the woman, but the entire
being of the man-child is saturated and permeated with the element of Christ. Hence, the man-child is the very constitution of
Christ....This man-child [can] be brought forth...by Christ's getting into part of the woman to constitute that part of her with all
the rich element of Christ. Do not consider this merely as an inter-
pretation, but apply it to your daily experience. Even if you submit
yourselves to Christ and receive something of Him, you are still the
woman and are not yet the man-child. You will not be strong until
you have allowed the element of Christ to be worked into your
being. The more the element of Christ is worked into you, the
stronger you will become. This is the man-child. (*Life-study of
Revelation,* pp. 414-415)

Today's Reading

According to the Bible, the seed of the woman will bruise the
head of the enemy. The seed of the woman in Genesis 3 primarily
refers to the Lord Jesus, but the overcomers also have a part in
this seed. The seed of the woman includes the church, especially
the overcomers. Even though the Lord bruised Satan's head, he is
still at work. The fulfillment of the seed of the woman bruising
Satan can be seen in the man-child in Revelation 12. The only
Overcomer includes all the overcomers (vv. 10-11).

When God changes His attitude towards a certain matter, He

makes a dispensational move. Every dispensational move brings in God's new way. His most important dispensational move is in Revelation 12. He wants to end this age and bring in the age of the kingdom....[Therefore], He must have His dispensational instrument. This is what God wants to do today.

The rapture of the man-child brings an end to the church age and introduces the kingdom age. The man-child enables God to move. If there is not a man-child and a rapture, God cannot make a dispensational move. We should never forget that God can be limited. He waits for man in all of His moves.

Of all the dispensational moves, the man-child is the greatest because it removes man's power and the devil's power, and it brings in the kingdom. We live in the most privileged time; we can do the most for God. *Light will show us the way, but strength and power will enable us to walk the road.* (Watchman Nee, *The Glorious Church,* pp. 153, 157)

The fighting of the overcoming believers against Satan is to usher in God's kingdom. The Lord teaches us to pray for the coming of the kingdom (Matt. 6:10). Along with our prayer for the kingdom's coming, we need to fight for it.

The rapture of the man-child to heaven, the casting of Satan to earth, and the declaration in heaven signify that the man-child will bring the kingdom to earth. When the man-child is raptured to heaven and Satan is cast down from heaven to earth, that will be the time for the kingdom of God to come. Not only will the kingdom come, but also the salvation of our God. Although we have God's salvation today, we do not yet enjoy it in full, to the uttermost. But when the kingdom of God comes, we shall enjoy God's salvation in full. It is the same with the power of God and the authority of Christ. We have participated in God's power and Christ's authority today, but our full enjoyment of them will be in the kingdom age. (*Life-study of Revelation,* pp. 456-457)

Further Reading: Life-study of Revelation, msg. 45; *The Glorious Church,* Appendix

Enlightenment and inspiration: _____

_____

_____

_____

Hymns, #893

1   Conflict today is fierce,
         The strength of Satan more;
     The cry of battle calling now
         Is louder than before.
         The rebel voice of hell
         E'en stronger now becomes;
     But list, the midnight cry resounds,
         Behold, I quickly come!

2   Trials more bitter grow,
         The fighting doth enlarge;
     Hell's forces rally all their pow'rs
         And gather for the charge.
         Yet while we wait and watch
         And feel the war severe,
     We hear the joyful song ring out,
         Jesus, the Lord, is near!

3   'Tis harder at the end
         The word to testify,
     For Satan fights with all his pow'r
         Our witness to defy.
         Much greater strength we need
         The foe to overcome;
     How happy when the Lord we see
         And all our sighing's done!

4   Who then will forward go
         Strong in His mighty power?
     Who then will firmly trust the Lord
         Until the vict'ry hour;
         Till with the conqu'rors blest,
         The triumph song's begun?
     That man will then rejoice to hear,
         Behold, I quickly come!

5   Who then will choose God's best,
         And take the narrow track,
     Though passing thru the wildest storms,
         Yet never turning back?
         Who now will dare press on,
         Enduring pain and fear?
     All such will then rejoice to see
         Jesus, the Lord, is near!

6   Though deep the darkness be
       We still would onward go,
   Till we the day of rapture greet
       And glory 'round shall glow.
       'Tis there we'll see the Lord,
       And Satan overcome;
   The overcomers will rejoice,
       Jesus, the Lord, has come!

Composition for prophecy with main point and sub-points: _____

_____

_____

_____

_____

_____

_____

_____

_____

_____

_____

_____

_____

_____

_____

_____

_____

_____

_____

_____

_____

_____

_____

_____

_____

_____

_____

_____

**Closely Following the Present Vision
of the Lord's Recovery
by Holding to the Teaching of the Apostles
to Remain in the Essence of Oneness**

Scripture Reading: 1 Tim. 1:3-4; Titus 1:9; Rom. 15:6; 1 Cor.
1:10; John 17:11, 21-23

Day 1 I. **We must closely follow the present vision of
the Lord's recovery by holding to the teach-
ing of the apostles, the teaching of God's eternal economy; this teaching is the holding
factor of the one accord (Titus 1:9; Acts 2:42a,
46a; 1 Tim. 1:3-4; 4:6; 2 Tim. 3:10; Eph. 1:10; 3:9):**

A. The central vision of God in the entire Bible is
the vision of God's economy, which is God working Himself through His Divine Trinity into
man, in order that man would enjoy the riches of
Christ to become His members and be constituted into the Body of Christ for the manifestation of the Triune God (vv. 8-11, 16-21; 4:4-6).

B. The one thing, the unique thing, in the Lord's
recovery is God's eternal economy with Christ
as the centrality and universality (Col. 3:10-11).

C. The content of God's eternal economy is Christ;
actually, Christ Himself in His full ministry of
three stages is the divine economy (John 1:14;
1 Cor. 15:45b; Rev. 1:4; 3:1; 4:5; 5:6):

1. Christ is the hub (the center), the spokes
(the support), and the rim (the circumference) of the great wheel of God's economy
(Col. 1:17; Ezek. 1:15).

2. Our thinking should be focused on the excel-
lency of the knowledge and experience of
Christ; focusing on anything other than
this "one thing" causes us to think differently, thus creating dissensions among us
(Phil. 2:2; 3:8, 12-14; Luke 10:41b-42; Psa.
27:4).

Day 2 D. Various strange teachings other than the
unique teaching of the eternal economy of God
are always used by Satan to cause dissension
and even division in the church (Heb. 13:9a;
1 Tim. 1:3-4; 6:3-4).

E. Any teaching, even a scriptural one, that dis-
tracts us from Christ and the church is a wind
that carries us away from God's central purpose
(Eph. 4:14):
1. What we teach should not be measured by
whether or not it is scriptural; it must be
measured by whether or not it is divisive.
2. The winds of teaching overthrow the faith
of some believers, frustrate the building up
of the Body of Christ, and divide the members of the organic Body of Christ (2 Tim.
2:18; 1 Cor. 1:10-11).

F. The one thing that should be focused on, stressed,
and ministered in the Lord's recovery is the eternal economy of God; only one kind of ministry
builds up and never divides—this is the unique
ministry of God's economy (1 Tim. 1:3-4):
1. "Human pride always likes to make the self
different from others. You may speak one
thing, but I would never speak what you
speak because of my pride. I want to speak
something different from what you speak,
something new and something better. This
is the self, and this is fleshly pride" (*The
Divine Economy,* p. 124).
2. The only way that we can be preserved in
the eternal oneness for the one new man is
to teach the same thing—the economy of
God (Rom. 15:6).

Day 3 II. **We need to consider *one new man* in Ephesians 2:15 together with *one mouth* in Romans
15:6 and *speak the same thing* in 1 Corinthians
1:10:**
A. For the church as the one new man, we all need

to take Christ as our person in the matter of speaking (Matt. 12:34-37; Eph. 3:17a; John 7:16-18; 8:28, 38a; 12:49-50; 14:10).

B. There is only one new man, and the one new man has only one person, so the one new man speaks with one mouth and says the same thing (Col. 3:10-11; Heb. 1:1-2a; cf. Gen. 11:7, 9).

C. *With one accord* and *with one mouth* (Rom. 15:6) mean that even though we are many and all are speaking, we all *speak the same thing* (1 Cor. 1:10).

D. The church is the one new man with only one person—Christ; this person controls our speaking; thus, whatever He speaks is surely *the same thing*.

E. In the one new man there is only one person, and only this person has the freedom to speak (Matt. 17:5):

   1. In the one new man there is no freedom for us to speak our own things.

   2. The Lord Jesus has the absolute freedom to speak, and our natural man has absolutely no freedom to speak.

F. Although we are many and come from many places, we all have one mouth and we all speak the same thing; this is because we all are the one new man having only one person (Eph. 2:15; 4:22-24; 3:17a; 2 Cor. 2:10).

Day 4 III. **The oneness in God's economy is preserved by life and light, which are the essence of oneness:**

A. Ezekiel 37 reveals that when we are gathered together in oneness, we receive the breathing of God as life and the speaking of God as light (vv. 1-14):

   1. The unique way to have the Body of Christ in the genuine oneness is the way of life (Matt. 7:13-14; Rev. 22:1; John 10:10a; 1:4; 8:12; Col. 2:19).

2. God speaks out of the Tent of Meeting on the ground of oneness; His speaking brings in light, and light issues in life; we have light because we are on the ground of oneness (Lev. 1:1; Exo. 25:22; cf. Rom. 3:25).

3. Light, life, and oneness are a cycle—the more light, the more life; the more life, the more oneness; and the more oneness, the more light (1 John 1:1-9).

B. Psalm 133 says that *there,* upon the oneness, the Lord commands the blessing—life forever; if we would remain in the oneness, we must remain in life, because life maintains the oneness (v. 3).

Day 5

C. John 17 reveals that the essence of oneness is life and light:

1. To be kept in the Father's name is to be kept by and in His life; only those who are born of the Father and have the Father's life can participate in the Father's name (v. 11).

2. To be sanctified in the Father's word, the truth, is a matter of light; the sanctifying truth is the shining of the light, by which we move out of ourselves and into the Triune God (vv. 17, 21).

3. To be perfected in the Father's glory is to be brought into the enjoyment of the God of glory in a corporate, built-up way to arrive at the oneness in the Triune God for His radiant expression (vv. 22-23; Eph. 4:11-13).

D. Revelation 21 and 22 reveal that life and light are the essence of the oneness of the New Jerusalem (21:23; 22:1-2, 14, 17).

IV. **Oneness keeps us from evil, whereas division opens the door to evil:**

A. Oneness is all-inclusive; it includes God the Father, Christ the Lord, the Spirit as the Giver of life, and every positive blessing (Psa. 133; Eph. 1:3; 4:4-6).

B. Division is all-inclusive; it includes Satan, sin, worldliness, the flesh, the self, the old man, evil temper, and every negative thing (Rom. 16:17-18; Jude 19).

C. The New Jerusalem will be the ultimate consummation of oneness and of all the positive things included in it, but the lake of fire will be the ultimate reservoir of division and of all the negative things included in it (Rev. 21:2; 20:10).

Day 6   V. **In order to remain in the essence of oneness, we must reject our self-choice and self-preference; the divisions among God's people are the result of having different preferences (Deut. 12:5, 8, 13, 17; 1 Cor. 1:10-12):**

A. The children of Israel were not allowed to worship God and enjoy the offerings in the place of their choice; this was for the keeping of the oneness of God's people, thus avoiding the division caused by man's preference (Deut. 12:8, 13, 17; cf. John 4:24; Eph. 4:3; 1 Cor. 1:10).

B. In the distribution of the good land, Reuben and Gad exercised their own choice regarding their portion of the land (Num. 32:1-22):

1. Eventually, because they acted according to their own choice, their land was the first part of the land of Israel to be taken over by the Gentile invaders from the east (1 Chron. 5:25-26).

2. In spiritual matters it is much better not to act according to our choice but to leave matters in the hand of the Lord and let Him do what He wants according to His choice; we may think that our choice is the best, but actually it is the worst (cf. Gen. 13:5-18).

3. The two tribes made their request because of what they had (a very great abundance of livestock—Num. 32:1) and because of what they saw (a land good for livestock—v. 4):

a. This shows that self-choice comes from two things—considering what we have and need and considering how a particular situation or opportunity that we see in front of us fits in with our needs.

b. In the church life and in the Lord's work, we must resist the temptation of having our self-choice for taking care of our own welfare.

4. In serving the Lord, we need to learn to give up our own choice in order to avoid obligating ourselves to God and to His people (v. 22).

5. Reuben and Gad did not cross the river Jordan to receive the promise of the good land with the body of the children of Israel; this signifies our old man not being dealt with and buried and our receiving the enjoyment of Christ separately, without the Body of Christ.

6. We must learn not to follow the example of Reuben and Gad but to follow the pattern of the other tribes, who allowed the Lord to make the choice for them; in all that we do, we must be Body-conscious and Body-centered:

a. Every local church has its own administration, but whatever a local church does must be done with careful consideration of how this would affect the other churches as the local expressions of the entire Body.

b. We all must see that we are here for the Lord's recovery and that the Lord's recovery is of the Lord's one move by His one ministry to produce His unique Body for His unique testimony.

Morning Nourishment

Col.   And He is before all things, and all things cohere in
1:17-18   Him; and He is the Head of the Body, the church; He
is the beginning, the Firstborn from the dead, that
He Himself might have the first place in all things.

The one thing that should be focused on, stressed, and ministered in the Lord's recovery is the New Testament economy of
God. God's New Testament economy is "the thing."...I consider
the fifty-one messages I gave on God's New Testament economy
in 1984 as a consummation of what the Lord has shown us in His
recovery.

My concern is that many of you have never gotten into these
things and that you do not have any interest or any burden to
teach people these things. Instead you pick up one small item of the
recovery and make it a big item. We must realize...that "the thing"
in the Lord's recovery is the content of God's New Testament economy—the Triune God embodied, realized, and consummated and
taking the seven steps of incarnation, human living, crucifixion,
resurrection, breathing Himself into His believers, ascension, and
pouring Himself out to dispense Himself entirely into His people
as a Body. In the finalization of His New Testament economy in
the book of Revelation He is the seven Spirits, out from the eternal One, of the Redeemer, the intensification of the Triune God in
the overcoming church, consummating in the golden lampstands
and the New Jerusalem. We have to see this and we have to learn
how to minister these things. (*Elders' Training, Book 5: Fellowship concerning the Lord's Up-to-date Move,* pp. 21, 30-31)

Today's Reading

Justification by faith is not "the thing," but it is one item in
the Lord's progressive recovery of the basic truths. The matters
related to the inner life are wonderful but even the inner life is
not "the thing." Sanctification, the brotherhood, or the presby-
tery are not "the thing."...I am for baptism by immersion, but
immersion is not "the thing." Even the church practice is not
"the thing." (*Elders' Training, Book 5: Fellowship concerning the*

Lord's Up-to-date Move, pp. 30-31)

If we are to be the overcomers, we need to be clear about God's economy. Christ is the centrality and universality of the divine economy (Col. 3:10-11). Actually, God's economy is just Christ. What God desires to have is Christ. Christ is God's good pleasure and His unique goal.

The New Testament shows us this in Ephesians 1 and 3. These chapters speak of God's good pleasure (1:5, 9) and God's eternal purpose, God's heart's desire (3:11). God's good pleasure is Christ. A church without Christ as the centrality and universality is not pleasant to God. God could never be pleased with a church without Christ. God does not want to see merely a group of people meeting and serving together. He wants to see Christ among them, and He is concerned about how much Christ is among them. How much God would be pleased with us depends upon how much Christ we have. Everything we do must be in Christ, with Christ, by Christ, through Christ, and to Christ. (*The Satanic Chaos in the Old Creation and the Divine Economy for the New Creation,* p. 100)

According to the picture presented in Ezekiel 1, God's New Testament economy is like a great wheel, having Christ as its every part....Christ is the hub, the center, of God's New Testament economy. Colossians 1:17 says that "all things cohere in Him," which means to exist together by Christ as the holding center, just as the spokes of a wheel hold together by the hub at their center....Christ is also the spokes, the support, of the great wheel of God's New Testament economy....Furthermore, He is the rim, the circumference. This means that God's entire New Testament economy and His move in His economy are just Christ. (*Messages to the Trainees in Fall 1990,* p. 142)

Further Reading: The Vision of the Age, chs. 2-3; *Elders' Training, Book 5: Fellowship concerning the Lord's Up-to-date Move,* ch. 2; *The Satanic Chaos in the Old Creation and the Divine Economy for the New Creation,* chs. 1, 4; *Messages to the Trainees in Fall 1990,* ch. 18

Enlightenment and inspiration: _____

_____
_____
_____

Morning Nourishment

1 Tim. Even as I exhorted you, when I was going into Mac-
1:3-4 edonia, to remain in Ephesus in order that you
       might charge certain ones not to teach different
       things nor to give heed to myths and unending
       genealogies, which produce questionings rather
       than God's economy, which is in faith.
Rom.   That with one accord you may with one mouth glo-
15:6   rify the God and Father of our Lord Jesus Christ.

Paul tells Timothy in 1 Timothy 1:3 that he left him there in
Ephesus to charge certain ones not to teach different things....
[Then] Paul went on to tell Timothy what those ones who were
teaching different things should be occupied with—God's economy....There is only one ministry that ever builds up and that
never destroys—this is God's economy.

Please do not have the peace and assurance that as long as you
teach things scripturally that it is all right. It is not all right because
your teaching creates division. Even your right teaching creates
division. We all must realize that, generally speaking, the different
denominations do not teach anything wrong. They have all tried
and endeavored to teach the right things, the scriptural things.
Eventually, however, the Body of Christ has been cut into pieces.

We should be on the alert and watchful. We do not want the
right teaching. We want the teaching which teaches God's economy. Now we can understand Paul's charge in 1 Corinthians to
speak the same thing (1:10)....Whatever you teach should not be
measured by whether it is wrong or right. It must be measured by
whether it is divisive or not. Only one kind of ministry builds up
and never divides—this is the unique ministry of God's economy.
We must be reminded that Paul left Timothy in Ephesus with a
charge to tell certain ones not to teach different things and that
what they teach should be related to God's economy. (*Elders'
Training, Book 3: The Way to Carry Out the Vision,* pp. 43-46)

Today's Reading

The Body is a matter of being members one of another, but for the new man the requirements are even more than what the Body requires....Romans 15:6...says, "That with one accord you may with one mouth glorify...God."...How could so many Christians come together and have only one mouth?...The church is one new man. How many mouths does a man have? It has one. Not only are we all members one of another, but we also all speak with one mouth. Do you see how much is required of us? It is already restricting enough to be members one of another, and now even when we speak, we all have to have one mouth. This is not my word; it is Paul's word. How many mouths does the one new man have? One. Then who is the mouth? If you say that Christ is the mouth, you are too transcendent. In order to resolve this matter you must see that there is only one new man with only one person. In the whole body there is only one mouth, but who controls this mouth? It is the person who controls the mouth.

The church is not merely the Body but also the one new man. The Body needs Christ as its life, whereas the new man needs Christ as his person. When you want to speak, when I want to speak, when any one of us wants to speak, we must resolve the basic question: Who is the person that is speaking here? If you are the person, you have your own mouth. If I am the person, I have my own mouth. Thus, you have your mouth, and I have my mouth; therefore, there are two mouths. When each one is a person individually and each one speaks his own matters, we have many mouths. This is a society or a denomination, and this is the condition of today's degraded Christianity. In the Lord's recovery, however, the church is the Body, and the church is the one new man. The Body has Christ as life, and the new man has Christ as a person. When you speak, it is not you who are the person; when I speak, neither is it I. When anyone speaks, it is Christ who is the person. What is the result? The result is that there is only one mouth. (*One Body, One Spirit, and One New Man*, pp. 58-59)

Further Reading: Elders' Training, Book 3: The Way to Carry Out the Vision, ch. 4; One Body, One Spirit, and One New Man, ch. 5

Enlightenment and inspiration: _____

_____

_____

_____

Morning Nourishment

1 Cor. Now I beseech you, brothers, through the name of our
1:10 Lord Jesus Christ, that you all speak the same thing
and *that* there be no divisions among you, but *that* you
be attuned in the same mind and in the same opinion.
Rom. That with one accord you may with one mouth glorify
15:6 the God and Father of our Lord Jesus Christ.

In 1 Corinthians 1:10 Paul says that all "speak the same thing."
This verse greatly bothered me many years ago. I thought, "How
could all Christians speak the same thing?" It seemed to me that
this was impossible, but one day I understood. The church is the
one new man with only one person, and this person controls our
speaking, so whatever He speaks is surely "the same thing" that
we all speak as the new man.

Many preachers and pastors in today's Christianity are all
their own persons, all have their own mouths, and all speak their
own things. Therefore, they have many mouths, each speaking a
different thing. However, the church is not like this. The church is
the one new man with Christ as her person. Whenever the brothers and sisters are about to speak something, they do not take
themselves as the person; instead, they allow Christ to be the person. You let Christ be your person when you speak, and I let
Christ be my person when I speak. Eventually, everyone speaks
the same thing. (*One Body, One Spirit, and One New Man,* p. 59)

Today's Reading

The entire Bible has one mouth and speaks the same thing,
even though it was written over a long period of time by many different people in many different places....Although we are many
and we come from many places, all of us have one mouth, and we
all speak the same thing. This is because we all are the one new
man having only one person.

Many times I wanted to speak, but I checked within,..."Is it I
who want to speak or is it the Lord?"...In the matter of speaking,
is the Lord the person, or am I the person? If it is I, there will be a
problem; if it is the Lord, there will be no problem. If I allow the

Lord to be the person, He is the One who speaks; then…if you allow the Lord to be the person, you will speak the same thing that I have spoken. We have one mouth speaking the same thing.

There is, however, [a] condition in which people blindly follow others: I speak whatever you speak, and you speak whatever I speak. In this way we make a show to everyone that we all have only one mouth and we speak the same thing. You must see that… [this is a not right condition.] We do not want the condition in Christianity, nor do we want a condition of blindly following others. We want a condition in which the one new man speaks. There is only one new man, and this one new man has only one person, so the one new man speaks with one mouth and says the same thing.

You have to consider "one mouth" in Romans 15:6 and "speak the same thing" in 1 Corinthians 1:10 together with "one new man" in Ephesians 2:15. Otherwise, you will never understand the first two verses. You may wonder how the entire church can have only one mouth and how millions of members can speak the same thing. Humanly speaking, this is absolutely impossible. However, we must see that in Romans 15, Paul was speaking of a local church. In a local church, there must be only one mouth.… When there are many persons, there are many ideas; when there are many ideas, there are many opinions, but we thank the Lord that now there is one mouth and one person here. There are no policemen here; each of us is absolutely free, but on the other hand, you have absolutely no freedom because within you there is another person. You may be about to speak, but something "pinches" you from within, telling you not to say anything. All you can say is, "Thank the Lord!" When you want to speak again, the Lord pinches you again, so you simply say, "Amen!"…He is in all of us as one person. The person in you is the person who is in me. We all have only one person. Who is this person? This person is Christ. (*One Body, One Spirit, and One New Man,* pp. 60-63)

Further Reading: One Body, One Spirit, and One New Man, chs. 5, 7; *Elders' Training, Book 3: The Way to Carry Out the Vision,* ch. 12

Enlightenment and inspiration: _____
_____
_____
_____

Morning Nourishment

Lev. **Then Jehovah called to Moses and spoke to him out**
1:1 **of the Tent of Meeting...**
Psa. **Behold, how good and how pleasant it is for brothers**
133:1, 3 **to dwell in unity!...For there Jehovah commanded**
the blessing: Life forever.

When...the children of Israel made their exodus from Egypt and were brought into the wilderness, they built a tabernacle. God took up residence in this tabernacle, and as a result, it became the Tent of Meeting....Leviticus 1:1 indicates that the Lord spoke to Moses out of the Tent of Meeting. Thus, the tabernacle, the Tent of Meeting, became the center of God's oracle, of God's speaking. Almost the entire book of Leviticus is a record of the Lord's speaking out of the Tent of Meeting.

God's speaking is intimately related to the ground of oneness. If we are on this ground, which is the proper ground, we shall have God's speaking day by day. But if we do not have the speaking of God, then we probably do not have the ground of oneness.

According to the book of Leviticus, God spoke from the Holy of Holies. The book of Leviticus is the result of this kind of divine speaking. Hence, God spoke from oneness. When this oneness is lost, God's oracle is lost also.

God's speaking brings in light, and light issues in life. When we do not have God's speaking, we have death and darkness. Death and darkness damage the Body and cause the members to become detached. Today's Christianity is full of death and darkness because the genuine oneness in life is lacking. (*The Genuine Ground of Oneness,* pp. 22-23)

Today's Reading

We receive our light from the speaking God. In order to receive light, we need God's speaking on the proper ground of oneness. Today God is still speaking in the Tent of Meeting, that is, in the center of oneness and on the ground of oneness. The tent of meeting is the ground, the base, of oneness. It is in this place that God's word is spoken to enlighten us. Apart from God's speaking, we are in darkness. But when His word comes, we are in light. Where God's speaking is, there is always light.

In Psalm 36:9 the psalmist…[says], "For with You is the fountain of life; in Your light we see light." This verse is…related to the temple, [which was the continuation and enlargement of the Tent of Meeting]. Only in the temple could God's people enjoy the fountain of life. Furthermore, it was in the temple that they could see light in God's light. This is a further indication that the essence of the oneness of God's children is life and light.

This is confirmed by Psalm 133, which begins with the words, "Behold, how good and how pleasant it is for brothers to dwell in unity!" The psalm concludes like this: "For there Jehovah commanded the blessing: Life forever." As this psalm makes clear, the blessing of life is related to the oneness of God's people.

The principle applies today also. If we would be under the Lord's commanded blessing of life, we must be on the ground of oneness….God is neither narrow nor exclusive, but He is definite. He is definite regarding His principle and His economy….Verse 3 of Psalm 133 is very definite. Here the psalmist says that *there* upon the oneness, the Lord commands the blessing: Life forever.

It is crucial for us to see that the oneness among God's children is preserved by life and light….The more light we have, the more life we enjoy; the more life we enjoy, the more light we receive. Light, life, and oneness go together. The more light, the more life; the more life, the more oneness; and the more oneness, the more light. This cycle of light, life, and oneness preserves the oneness.

All the churches in the Lord's recovery must be in life and under the shining of light. By the shining of the light and through the watering and supply of the life, we are one….May we all be deeply impressed with the fact that oneness can be prevailing and can be preserved only by life and light. (*The Genuine Ground of Oneness,* pp. 23-28)

Further Reading: The Genuine Ground of Oneness, chs. 2-3, 10

Enlightenment and inspiration: _____

_____

_____

_____

Morning Nourishment

John ...Holy Father, keep them in Your name, which You
17:11 have given to Me, that they may be one even as We are.
  17 Sanctify them in the truth; Your word is truth.
  22 And the glory which You have given Me I have given
      to them, that they may be one, even as We are one.

[In John 17:11], to be kept in the Father's name is to be kept by His life, because only those who are born of the Father and have the Father's life can participate in the Father's name. The Son has given the Father's life to those whom the Father has given Him (v. 2). Hence, the believers enjoy the divine life as the essence of their oneness. If we are kept in the Father's life, we shall be preserved in the oneness.

To be sanctified [in verse 17] is to be separated unto God from the world....Here the Lord prays to the Father to sanctify the believers in the truth, which is the Father's word. As the Father's name is a matter of life, so the Father's truth is a matter of light. Life and light are, therefore, the very essence of oneness.

John 17:22 indicates that the Triune God with His glory keeps the oneness of the believers. We are not kept in oneness by teachings or doctrines. We are preserved in oneness by life and light. The Triune God Himself is the life, and His word with His speaking is the light. By this life and this light the oneness is maintained. (*The Genuine Ground of Oneness*, pp. 25-26)

Today's Reading

In the Bible there are two lines: the line of life and the line of death. These two lines come from the two sources that exist in the universe. One of these sources is God, and the other is the devil, Satan. Furthermore, each of these lines will have a particular issue, result. The line of life begins with the tree of life and ends with the New Jerusalem. The line of death begins from the tree of the knowledge of good and evil and, passing through the great Babylon, ends with the lake of fire. Oneness is on the line of life, originates with God, and issues in the New Jerusalem. Division, on the contrary, is on the line of death, originates with Satan, and issues in the great Babylon and, ultimately, the lake of fire. If we would see the great truth of oneness in the Bible, we need to be clear about these two sources, lines, and results. Then we shall know where oneness and division belong.

Division is all-inclusive. It comprises such negative things as Satan, sin, worldliness, the flesh, the self, the old man, and evil temper. If we are enlightened concerning the nature of division, we shall see that it includes every negative thing. Do not think that division stands by itself and that it is not related to such things as the flesh, the self, and worldliness. Division is not only related to all negative things; it includes all negative things.

Just as division is all-inclusive, so, in the same principle, oneness is all-inclusive. It includes God, Christ, and the Spirit. Ephesians 4:3-6 indicates this. In the oneness revealed in these verses, we have God the Father, Christ the Lord, and the Spirit as the Giver of life. This oneness includes such positive things as our regenerated spirit and our transformed and renewed mind. Everything positive is included in the proper oneness.

The New Jerusalem will be the ultimate consummation of oneness and of all the positive things included in it. But the lake of fire will be the ultimate reservoir of division and all the negative things included in it....The New Jerusalem...will be the ultimate consummation and expression of oneness. This city will be characterized by one throne, one river, one tree, and one street. In the street will flow the river of the water of life, and on either side of the river there will be the tree of life. Hence, we may properly call the one street of the New Jerusalem the street of life. This unique street will make division impossible. Division with all the negative things related to it will be found only in the lake of fire. (*The Genuine Ground of Oneness,* pp. 29-31)

Further Reading: The Genuine Ground of Oneness, ch. 3; *Truth Messages,* chs. 6-7; *The Building Up of the Body of Christ,* ch. 4

Enlightenment and inspiration: _____

_____

_____

_____

Morning Nourishment

Deut. 12:5 But to the place which Jehovah your God will choose out of all your tribes to put His name, to His habitation, shall you seek, and there shall you go.

Num. 32:5 And they said, If we have found favor in your sight, let this land be given to your servants for a possession; do not make us cross over the Jordan.

The request of the two tribes, Reuben and Gad (Num. 32:1-5), was not wrong, but neither was it right. Their desire was to receive what God had promised, according to their choice as the best, not according to God's choice as the best. The desire to receive what God had promised was not wrong. However, they were not right in wanting to receive this according to their choice as the best. Eventually, their land was the first part of the land of Israel to be taken over by the Gentile invaders from the east. The tribes of Reuben and Gad suffered, and this suffering was related to their having their own choice.

In spiritual matters it is terrible to do things according to our choice. Whatever is according to our choice will not turn out to be profitable. We may think that our choice is the best, but it is actually the worst. Therefore, in spiritual matters we should try not to act according to our choice. It is much better for us to leave matters in the hand of the Lord and let Him do according to His choice. (*Life-study of Numbers,* pp. 317-318)

Today's Reading

The two tribes made their request because of what they had (a very great multitude of cattle—v. 1) and because of what they saw (a land good for livestock—v. 4). This was the reason for their choice.

Self-choice, even in the church life, comes from two things—considering what we have and need and considering how a particular situation or opportunity that we see in front of us fits in with our needs. This should not be our situation in the church life or in the service of the Lord. Both in the church life and in the Lord's work, we need to resist the temptation to have our self-choice for the purpose of taking care of our own welfare.

We need to learn the lesson of not considering what we have or
what is in front of us but leaving our future in the hand of the
Lord....If you insist on having your own choice, be prepared to
suffer as a result. Our choice is not the best selection. We are
shortsighted and somewhat selfish, so it is difficult for us to be
pure in motive, desire, intention, goal, and purpose. We should be
willing to give up our choice and tell the Lord that we do not have
any choice of our own.

The land requested by Reuben and Gad could be reached
without crossing the river Jordan. Without crossing the Jordan
signifies without having the old man dealt with and buried. Only
after we have had the old man dealt with and buried are we in a
position to talk about possessing the good land for our enjoyment.

Reuben and Gad did not receive the promise of the good land
with the body of the children of Israel. This signifies receiving the
enjoyment of Christ separately, without the Body of Christ.

Often in making a choice a brother will care not for his wife but
for himself. He may say that he is for his wife, but deep in his
heart he is for himself. Likewise, as the elders from various
churches are having fellowship, the elders of each church may
stand for themselves and their interests, not for the other
churches, with each elder claiming that his concern is for the
Lord's purpose and the building up of the Body....It is difficult for
us not to have our own choice.

If in the Lord's recovery our standing is that we will not have
our own choice but leave the choice to the Lord, there will not be
any problems among us. However, if we have our own choice, there
will eventually be problems and suffering. Let us learn not to follow Reuben and Gad, but to follow the other tribes who allowed
the Lord to make the choice for them. Let us wait for the lot and
not have our own choice. (*Life-study of Numbers,* pp. 318-319, 322)

Further Reading: Life-study of Deuteronomy, msg. 11; *Life-study
of Numbers,* msg. 45; *Elders' Training, Book 4: Other Crucial
Matters concerning the Practice of the Lord's Recovery,* chs. 3-4

Enlightenment and inspiration: _____
_____
_____
_____

Hymns, #832

1   Christ the Son of God and His redemptive deed
     Are the saving faith which is our only creed.
     All the other doctrines do not faith comprise;
     Christ, His work and person, only qualifies.

2   All the other teachings used improperly
     Are the "winds of doctrine," spoiling unity:
     Blowing saints away from Christ who is the Head,
     Building not the Body, tearing down instead.

3   Thus we must relinquish doctrines of all kinds,
     Only keep the faith that oneness we may find.
     In the Lord the Spirit we are one indeed;
     Just to keep this oneness is our only need.

4   Truth we must be holding, which is Christ Himself,
     That we be delivered from the sects of self,
     That in all things growing into Christ the Head,
     Built will be the Body and to fulness led.

5   To the "unity of faith" we must attain,
     All the "winds of doctrine" evermore disdain;
     Holding Christ the Spirit, our reality,
     For the Body's growing in its unity.

Composition for prophecy with main point and sub-points: _____

_____
_____
_____
_____
_____
_____
_____
_____
_____
_____
_____
_____
_____
_____
_____
_____
_____
_____
_____
_____
_____
_____
_____
_____
_____
_____
_____
_____
_____
_____
_____
_____
_____
_____
_____
_____
_____
_____
_____

Reading Schedule for the Recovery Version of the Old Testament with Footnotes

Wk.	Lord's Day	Monday	Tuesday	Wednesday	Thursday	Friday	Saturday
1	☐ Gen 1:1-5	☐ 1:6-23	☐ 1:24-31	☐ 2:1-9	☐ 2:10-25	☐ 3:1-13	☐ 3:14-24
2	☐ 4:1-26	☐ 5:1-32	☐ 6:1-22	☐ 7:1—8:3	☐ 8:4-22	☐ 9:1-29	☐ 10:1-32
3	☐ 11:1-32	☐ 12:1-20	☐ 13:1-18	☐ 14:1-24	☐ 15:1-21	☐ 16:1-16	☐ 17:1-27
4	☐ 18:1-33	☐ 19:1-38	☐ 20:1-18	☐ 21:1-34	☐ 22:1-24	☐ 23:1—24:27	☐ 24:28-67
5	☐ 25:1-34	☐ 26:1-35	☐ 27:1-46	☐ 28:1-22	☐ 29:1-35	☐ 30:1-43	☐ 31:1-55
6	☐ 32:1-32	☐ 33:1—34:31	☐ 35:1-29	☐ 36:1-43	☐ 37:1-36	☐ 38:1—39:23	☐ 40:1—41:13
7	☐ 41:14-57	☐ 42:1-38	☐ 43:1-34	☐ 44:1-34	☐ 45:1-28	☐ 46:1-34	☐ 47:1-31
8	☐ 48:1-22	☐ 49:1-15	☐ 49:16-33	☐ 50:1-26	☐ Exo 1:1-22	☐ 2:1-25	☐ 3:1-22
9	☐ 4:1-31	☐ 5:1-23	☐ 6:1-30	☐ 7:1-25	☐ 8:1-32	☐ 9:1-35	☐ 10:1-29
10	☐ 11:1-10	☐ 12:1-14	☐ 12:15-36	☐ 12:37-51	☐ 13:1-22	☐ 14:1-31	☐ 15:1-27
11	☐ 16:1-36	☐ 17:1-16	☐ 18:1-27	☐ 19:1-25	☐ 20:1-26	☐ 21:1-36	☐ 22:1-31
12	☐ 23:1-33	☐ 24:1-18	☐ 25:1-22	☐ 25:23-40	☐ 26:1-14	☐ 26:15-37	☐ 27:1-21
13	☐ 28:1-21	☐ 28:22-43	☐ 29:1-21	☐ 29:22-46	☐ 30:1-10	☐ 30:11-38	☐ 31:1-17
14	☐ 31:18—32:35	☐ 33:1-23	☐ 34:1-35	☐ 35:1-35	☐ 36:1-38	☐ 37:1-29	☐ 38:1-31
15	☐ 39:1-43	☐ 40:1-38	☐ Lev 1:1-17	☐ 2:1-16	☐ 3:1-17	☐ 4:1-35	☐ 5:1-19
16	☐ 6:1-30	☐ 7:1-38	☐ 8:1-36	☐ 9:1-24	☐ 10:1-20	☐ 11:1-47	☐ 12:1-8
17	☐ 13:1-28	☐ 13:29-59	☐ 14:1-18	☐ 14:19-32	☐ 14:33-57	☐ 15:1-33	☐ 16:1-17
18	☐ 16:18-34	☐ 17:1-16	☐ 18:1-30	☐ 19:1-37	☐ 20:1-27	☐ 21:1-24	☐ 22:1-33
19	☐ 23:1-22	☐ 23:23-44	☐ 24:1-23	☐ 25:1-23	☐ 25:24-55	☐ 26:1-24	☐ 26:25-46
20	☐ 27:1-34	☐ Num 1:1-54	☐ 2:1-34	☐ 3:1-51	☐ 4:1-49	☐ 5:1-31	☐ 6:1-27
21	☐ 7:1-41	☐ 7:42-88	☐ 7:89—8:26	☐ 9:1-23	☐ 10:1-36	☐ 11:1-35	☐ 12:1—13:33
22	☐ 14:1-45	☐ 15:1-41	☐ 16:1-50	☐ 17:1—18:7	☐ 18:8-32	☐ 19:1-22	☐ 20:1-29
23	☐ 21:1-35	☐ 22:1-41	☐ 23:1-30	☐ 24:1-25	☐ 25:1-18	☐ 26:1-65	☐ 27:1-23
24	☐ 28:1-31	☐ 29:1-40	☐ 30:1—31:24	☐ 31:25-54	☐ 32:1-42	☐ 33:1-56	☐ 34:1-29
25	☐ 35:1-34	☐ 36:1-13	☐ Deut 1:1-46	☐ 2:1-37	☐ 3:1-29	☐ 4:1-49	☐ 5:1-33
26	☐ 6:1—7:26	☐ 8:1-20	☐ 9:1-29	☐ 10:1-22	☐ 11:1-32	☐ 12:1-32	☐ 13:1—14:21

Reading Schedule for the Recovery Version of the Old Testament with Footnotes

Wk.	Lord's Day	Monday	Tuesday	Wednesday	Thursday	Friday	Saturday
27	☐ 14:22—15:23	☐ 16:1-22	☐ 17:1—18:8	☐ 18:9—19:21	☐ 20:1—21:17	☐ 21:18—22:30	☐ 23:1-25
28	☐ 24:1-22	☐ 25:1-19	☐ 26:1-19	☐ 27:1-26	☐ 28:1-68	☐ 29:1-29	☐ 30:1—31:29
29	☐ 31:30—32:52	☐ 33:1-29	☐ 34:1-12	☐ Josh 1:1-18	☐ 2:1-24	☐ 3:1-17	☐ 4:1-24
30	☐ 5:1-15	☐ 6:1-27	☐ 7:1-26	☐ 8:1-35	☐ 9:1-27	☐ 10:1-43	☐ 11:1—12:24
31	☐ 13:1-33	☐ 14:1—15:63	☐ 16:1—18:28	☐ 19:1-51	☐ 20:1—21:45	☐ 22:1-34	☐ 23:1—24:33
32	☐ Judg 1:1-36	☐ 2:1-23	☐ 3:1-31	☐ 4:1-24	☐ 5:1-31	☐ 6:1-40	☐ 7:1-25
33	☐ 8:1-35	☐ 9:1-57	☐ 10:1—11:40	☐ 12:1—13:25	☐ 14:1—15:20	☐ 16:1-31	☐ 17:1—18:31
34	☐ 19:1-30	☐ 20:1-48	☐ 21:1-25	☐ Ruth 1:1-22	☐ 2:1-23	☐ 3:1-18	☐ 4:1-22
35	☐ 1 Sam 1:1-28	☐ 2:1-36	☐ 3:1—4:22	☐ 5:1—6:21	☐ 7:1—8:22	☐ 9:1-27	☐ 10:1—11:15
36	☐ 12:1—13:23	☐ 14:1-52	☐ 15:1-35	☐ 16:1-23	☐ 17:1-58	☐ 18:1-30	☐ 19:1-24
37	☐ 20:1-42	☐ 21:1—22:23	☐ 23:1—24:22	☐ 25:1-44	☐ 26:1-25	☐ 27:1—28:25	☐ 29:1—30:31
38	☐ 31:1-13	☐ 2 Sam 1:1-27	☐ 2:1-32	☐ 3:1-39	☐ 4:1—5:25	☐ 6:1-23	☐ 7:1-29
39	☐ 8:1—9:13	☐ 10:1—11:27	☐ 12:1-31	☐ 13:1-39	☐ 14:1-33	☐ 15:1—16:23	☐ 17:1—18:33
40	☐ 19:1-43	☐ 20:1—21:22	☐ 22:1-51	☐ 23:1-39	☐ 24:1-25	☐ 1 Kings 1:1-19	☐ 1:20-53
41	☐ 2:1-46	☐ 3:1-28	☐ 4:1-34	☐ 5:1—6:38	☐ 7:1-22	☐ 7:23-51	☐ 8:1-36
42	☐ 8:37-66	☐ 9:1-28	☐ 10:1-29	☐ 11:1-43	☐ 12:1-33	☐ 13:1-34	☐ 14:1-31
43	☐ 15:1-34	☐ 16:1—17:24	☐ 18:1-46	☐ 19:1-21	☐ 20:1-43	☐ 21:1—22:53	☐ 2 Kings 1:1-18
44	☐ 2:1—3:27	☐ 4:1-44	☐ 5:1—6:33	☐ 7:1-20	☐ 8:1-29	☐ 9:1-37	☐ 10:1-36
45	☐ 11:1—12:21	☐ 13:1—14:29	☐ 15:1-38	☐ 16:1-20	☐ 17:1-41	☐ 18:1-37	☐ 19:1-37
46	☐ 20:1—21:26	☐ 22:1-20	☐ 23:1-37	☐ 24:1—25:30	☐ 1 Chron 1:1-54	☐ 2:1—3:24	☐ 4:1—5:26
47	☐ 6:1-81	☐ 7:1-40	☐ 8:1-40	☐ 9:1-44	☐ 10:1—11:47	☐ 12:1-40	☐ 13:1—14:17
48	☐ 15:1—16:43	☐ 17:1-27	☐ 18:1—19:19	☐ 20:1—21:30	☐ 22:1—23:32	☐ 24:1—25:31	☐ 26:1-32
49	☐ 27:1-34	☐ 28:1—29:30	☐ 2 Chron 1:1-17	☐ 2:1—3:17	☐ 4:1—5:14	☐ 6:1-42	☐ 7:1—8:18
50	☐ 9:1—10:19	☐ 11:1—12:16	☐ 13:1—15:19	☐ 16:1—17:19	☐ 18:1—19:11	☐ 20:1-37	☐ 21:1—22:12
51	☐ 23:1—24:27	☐ 25:1—26:23	☐ 27:1—28:27	☐ 29:1-36	☐ 30:1—31:21	☐ 32:1-33	☐ 33:1—34:33
52	☐ 35:1—36:23	☐ Ezra 1:1-11	☐ 2:1-70	☐ 3:1—4:24	☐ 5:1—6:22	☐ 7:1-28	☐ 8:1-36

Reading Schedule for the Recovery Version of the Old Testament with Footnotes

Wk.	Lord's Day	Monday	Tuesday	Wednesday	Thursday	Friday	Saturday
53	☐ 9:1—10:44	☐ Neh 1:1-11	☐ 2:1—3:32	☐ 4:1—5:19	☐ 6:1-19	☐ 7:1-73	☐ 8:1-18
54	☐ 9:1-20	☐ 9:21-38	☐ 10:1—11:36	☐ 12:1-47	☐ 13:1-31	☐ Esth 1:1-22	☐ 2:1—3:15
55	☐ 4:1—5:14	☐ 6:1—7:10	☐ 8:1-17	☐ 9:1—10:3	☐ Job 1:1-22	☐ 2:1—3:26	☐ 4:1—5:27
56	☐ 6:1—7:21	☐ 8:1—9:35	☐ 10:1—11:20	☐ 12:1—13:28	☐ 14:1—15:35	☐ 16:1—17:16	☐ 18:1—19:29
57	☐ 20:1—21:34	☐ 22:1—23:17	☐ 24:1—25:6	☐ 26:1—27:23	☐ 28:1—29:25	☐ 30:1—31:40	☐ 32:1—33:33
58	☐ 34:1—35:16	☐ 36:1-33	☐ 37:1-24	☐ 38:1-41	☐ 39:1-30	☐ 40:1-24	☐ 41:1-34
59	☐ 42:1-17	☐ Psa 1:1-6	☐ 2:1—3:8	☐ 4:1—6:10	☐ 7:1—8:9	☐ 9:1—10:18	☐ 11:1—15:5
60	☐ 16:1—17:15	☐ 18:1-50	☐ 19:1—21:13	☐ 22:1-31	☐ 23:1—24:10	☐ 25:1—27:14	☐ 28:1—30:12
61	☐ 31:1—32:11	☐ 33:1—34:22	☐ 35:1—36:12	☐ 37:1-40	☐ 38:1—39:13	☐ 40:1—41:13	☐ 42:1—43:5
62	☐ 44:1-26	☐ 45:1-17	☐ 46:1—48:14	☐ 49:1—50:23	☐ 51:1—52:9	☐ 53:1—55:23	☐ 56:1—58:11
63	☐ 59:1—61:8	☐ 62:1—64:10	☐ 65:1—67:7	☐ 68:1-35	☐ 69:1—70:5	☐ 71:1—72:20	☐ 73:1—74:23
64	☐ 75:1—77:20	☐ 78:1-72	☐ 79:1—81:16	☐ 82:1—84:12	☐ 85:1—87:7	☐ 88:1—89:52	☐ 90:1—91:16
65	☐ 92:1—94:23	☐ 95:1—97:12	☐ 98:1—101:8	☐ 102:1—103:22	☐ 104:1—105:45	☐ 106:1-48	☐ 107:1-43
66	☐ 108:1—109:31	☐ 110:1—112:10	☐ 113:1—115:18	☐ 116:1—118:29	☐ 119:1-32	☐ 119:33-72	☐ 119:73-120
67	☐ 119:121-176	☐ 120:1—124:8	☐ 125:1—128:6	☐ 129:1—132:18	☐ 133:1—135:21	☐ 136:1—138:8	☐ 139:1—140:13
68	☐ 141:1—144:15	☐ 145:1—147:20	☐ 148:1—150:6	☐ Prov 1:1-33	☐ 2:1—3:35	☐ 4:1—5:23	☐ 6:1-35
69	☐ 7:1—8:36	☐ 9:1—10:32	☐ 11:1—12:28	☐ 13:1—14:35	☐ 15:1-33	☐ 16:1-33	☐ 17:1-28
70	☐ 18:1-24	☐ 19:1—20:30	☐ 21:1—22:29	☐ 23:1-35	☐ 24:1—25:28	☐ 26:1—27:27	☐ 28:1—29:27
71	☐ 30:1-33	☐ 31:1-31	☐ Eccl 1:1-18	☐ 2:1—3:22	☐ 4:1—5:20	☐ 6:1—7:29	☐ 8:1—9:18
72	☐ 10:1—11:10	☐ 12:1-14	☐ S.S 1:1-8	☐ 1:9-17	☐ 2:1-17	☐ 3:1-11	☐ 4:1-8
73	☐ 4:9-16	☐ 5:1-16	☐ 6:1-13	☐ 7:1-13	☐ 8:1-14	☐ Isa 1:1-11	☐ 1:12-31
74	☐ 2:1-22	☐ 3:1-26	☐ 4:1-6	☐ 5:1-30	☐ 6:1-13	☐ 7:1-25	☐ 8:1-22
75	☐ 9:1-21	☐ 10:1-34	☐ 11:1—12:6	☐ 13:1-22	☐ 14:1-14	☐ 14:15-32	☐ 15:1—16:14
76	☐ 17:1—18:7	☐ 19:1-25	☐ 20:1—21:17	☐ 22:1-25	☐ 23:1-18	☐ 24:1-23	☐ 25:1-12
77	☐ 26:1-21	☐ 27:1-13	☐ 28:1-29	☐ 29:1-24	☐ 30:1-33	☐ 31:1—32:20	☐ 33:1-24
78	☐ 34:1-17	☐ 35:1-10	☐ 36:1-22	☐ 37:1-38	☐ 38:1—39:8	☐ 40:1-31	☐ 41:1-29

Reading Schedule for the Recovery Version of the Old Testament with Footnotes

Wk.	Lord's Day	Monday	Tuesday	Wednesday	Thursday	Friday	Saturday
79	42:1-25	43:1-28	44:1-28	45:1-25	46:1-13	47:1-15	48:1-22
80	49:1-13	49:14-26	50:1—51:23	52:1-15	53:1-12	54:1-17	55:1-13
81	56:1-12	57:1-21	58:1-14	59:1-21	60:1-22	61:1-11	62:1-12
82	63:1-19	64:1-12	65:1-25	66:1-24	Jer 1:1-19	2:1-19	2:20-37
83	3:1-25	4:1-31	5:1-31	6:1-30	7:1-34	8:1-22	9:1-26
84	10:1-25	11:1—12:17	13:1-27	14:1-22	15:1-21	16:1—17:27	18:1-23
85	19:1—20:18	21:1—22:30	23:1-40	24:1—25:38	26:1—27:22	28:1—29:32	30:1-24
86	31:1-23	31:24-40	32:1-44	33:1-26	34:1-22	35:1-19	36:1-32
87	37:1-21	38:1-28	39:1—40:16	41:1—42:22	43:1—44:30	45:1—46:28	47:1—48:16
88	48:17-47	49:1-22	49:23-39	50:1-27	50:28-46	51:1-27	51:28-64
89	52:1-34	Lam 1:1-22	2:1-22	3:1-39	3:40-66	4:1-22	5:1-22
90	Ezek 1:1-14	1:15-28	2:1—3:27	4:1—5:17	6:1—7:27	8:1—9:11	10:1—11:25
91	12:1—13:23	14:1—15:8	16:1-63	17:1—18:32	19:1-14	20:1-49	21:1-32
92	22:1-31	23:1-49	24:1-27	25:1—26:21	27:1-36	28:1-26	29:1—30:26
93	31:1—32:32	33:1-33	34:1-31	35:1—36:21	36:22-38	37:1-28	38:1—39:29
94	40:1-27	40:28-49	41:1-26	42:1—43:27	44:1-31	45:1-25	46:1-24
95	47:1-23	48:1-35	Dan 1:1-21	2:1-30	2:31-49	3:1-30	4:1-37
96	5:1-31	6:1-28	7:1-12	7:13-28	8:1-27	9:1-27	10:1-21
97	11:1-22	11:23-45	12:1-13	Hosea 1:1-11	2:1-23	3:1—4:19	5:1-15
98	6:1-11	7:1-16	8:1-14	9:1-17	10:1-15	11:1-12	12:1-14
99	13:1—14:9	Joel 1:1-20	2:1-16	2:17-32	3:1-21	Amos 1:1-15	2:1-16
100	3:1-15	4:1—5:27	6:1—7:17	8:1—9:15	Obad 1-21	Jonah 1:1-17	2:1—4:11
101	Micah 1:1-16	2:1—3:12	4:1—5:15	6:1—7:20	Nahum 1:1-15	2:1—3:19	Hab 1:1-17
102	2:1-20	3:1-19	Zeph 1:1-18	2:1-15	3:1-20	Hag 1:1-15	2:1-23
103	Zech 1:1-21	2:1-13	3:1-10	4:1-14	5:1—6:15	7:1—8:23	9:1-17
104	10:1—11:17	12:1—13:9	14:1-21	Mal 1:1-14	2:1-17	3:1-18	4:1-6

Reading Schedule for the Recovery Version of the New Testament with Footnotes

Wk.	Lord's Day	Monday	Tuesday	Wednesday	Thursday	Friday	Saturday
1	☐ Matt 1:1-2	☐ 1:3-7	☐ 1:8-17	☐ 1:18-25	☐ 2:1-23	☐ 3:1-6	☐ 3:7-17
2	☐ 4:1-11	☐ 4:12-25	☐ 5:1-4	☐ 5:5-12	☐ 5:13-20	☐ 5:21-26	☐ 5:27-48
3	☐ 6:1-8	☐ 6:9-18	☐ 6:19-34	☐ 7:1-12	☐ 7:13-29	☐ 8:1-13	☐ 8:14-22
4	☐ 8:23-34	☐ 9:1-13	☐ 9:14-17	☐ 9:18-34	☐ 9:35—10:5	☐ 10:6-25	☐ 10:26-42
5	☐ 11:1-15	☐ 11:16-30	☐ 12:1-14	☐ 12:15-32	☐ 12:33-42	☐ 12:43—13:2	☐ 13:3-12
6	☐ 13:13-30	☐ 13:31-43	☐ 13:44-58	☐ 14:1-13	☐ 14:14-21	☐ 14:22-36	☐ 15:1-20
7	☐ 15:21-31	☐ 15:32-39	☐ 16:1-12	☐ 16:13-20	☐ 16:21-28	☐ 17:1-13	☐ 17:14-27
8	☐ 18:1-14	☐ 18:15-22	☐ 18:23-35	☐ 19:1-15	☐ 19:16-30	☐ 20:1-16	☐ 20:17-34
9	☐ 21:1-11	☐ 21:12-22	☐ 21:23-32	☐ 21:33-46	☐ 22:1-22	☐ 22:23-33	☐ 22:34-46
10	☐ 23:1-12	☐ 23:13-39	☐ 24:1-14	☐ 24:15-31	☐ 24:32-51	☐ 25:1-13	☐ 25:14-30
11	☐ 25:31-46	☐ 26:1-16	☐ 26:17-35	☐ 26:36-46	☐ 26:47-64	☐ 26:65-75	☐ 27:1-26
12	☐ 27:27-44	☐ 27:45-56	☐ 27:57—28:15	☐ 28:16-20	☐ Mark 1:1	☐ 1:2-6	☐ 1:7-13
13	☐ 1:14-28	☐ 1:29-45	☐ 2:1-12	☐ 2:13-28	☐ 3:1-19	☐ 3:20-35	☐ 4:1-25
14	☐ 4:26-41	☐ 5:1-20	☐ 5:21-43	☐ 6:1-29	☐ 6:30-56	☐ 7:1-23	☐ 7:24-37
15	☐ 8:1-26	☐ 8:27—9:1	☐ 9:2-29	☐ 9:30-50	☐ 10:1-16	☐ 10:17-34	☐ 10:35-52
16	☐ 11:1-16	☐ 11:17-33	☐ 12:1-27	☐ 12:28-44	☐ 13:1-13	☐ 13:14-37	☐ 14:1-26
17	☐ 14:27-52	☐ 14:53-72	☐ 15:1-15	☐ 15:16-47	☐ 16:1-8	☐ 16:9-20	☐ Luke 1:1-4
18	☐ 1:5-25	☐ 1:26-46	☐ 1:47-56	☐ 1:57-80	☐ 2:1-8	☐ 2:9-20	☐ 2:21-39
19	☐ 2:40-52	☐ 3:1-20	☐ 3:21-38	☐ 4:1-13	☐ 4:14-30	☐ 4:31-44	☐ 5:1-26
20	☐ 5:27—6:16	☐ 6:17-38	☐ 6:39-49	☐ 7:1-17	☐ 7:18-23	☐ 7:24-35	☐ 7:36-50
21	☐ 8:1-15	☐ 8:16-25	☐ 8:26-39	☐ 8:40-56	☐ 9:1-17	☐ 9:18-26	☐ 9:27-36
22	☐ 9:37-50	☐ 9:51-62	☐ 10:1-11	☐ 10:12-24	☐ 10:25-37	☐ 10:38-42	☐ 11:1-13
23	☐ 11:14-26	☐ 11:27-36	☐ 11:37-54	☐ 12:1-12	☐ 12:13-21	☐ 12:22-34	☐ 12:35-48
24	☐ 12:49-59	☐ 13:1-9	☐ 13:10-17	☐ 13:18-30	☐ 13:31—14:6	☐ 14:7-14	☐ 14:15-24
25	☐ 14:25-35	☐ 15:1-10	☐ 15:11-21	☐ 15:22-32	☐ 16:1-13	☐ 16:14-22	☐ 16:23-31
26	☐ 17:1-19	☐ 17:20-37	☐ 18:1-14	☐ 18:15-30	☐ 18:31-43	☐ 19:1-10	☐ 19:11-27

Reading Schedule for the Recovery Version of the New Testament with Footnotes

Wk.	Lord's Day	Monday	Tuesday	Wednesday	Thursday	Friday	Saturday
27	□ Luke 19:28-48	□ 20:1-19	□ 20:20-38	□ 20:39—21:4	□ 21:5-27	□ 21:28-38	□ 22:1-20
28	□ 22:21-38	□ 22:39-54	□ 22:55-71	□ 23:1-43	□ 23:44-56	□ 24:1-12	□ 24:13-35
29	□ 24:36-53	□ John 1:1-13	□ 1:14-18	□ 1:19-34	□ 1:35-51	□ 2:1-11	□ 2:12-22
30	□ 2:23—3:13	□ 3:14-21	□ 3:22-36	□ 4:1-14	□ 4:15-26	□ 4:27-42	□ 4:43-54
31	□ 5:1-16	□ 5:17-30	□ 5:31-47	□ 6:1-15	□ 6:16-31	□ 6:32-51	□ 6:52-71
32	□ 7:1-9	□ 7:10-24	□ 7:25-36	□ 7:37-52	□ 7:53—8:11	□ 8:12-27	□ 8:28-44
33	□ 8:45-59	□ 9:1-13	□ 9:14-34	□ 9:35—10:9	□ 10:10-30	□ 10:31—11:4	□ 11:5-22
34	□ 11:23-40	□ 11:41-57	□ 12:1-11	□ 12:12-24	□ 12:25-36	□ 12:37-50	□ 13:1-11
35	□ 13:12-30	□ 13:31-38	□ 14:1-6	□ 14:7-20	□ 14:21-31	□ 15:1-11	□ 15:12-27
36	□ 16:1-15	□ 16:16-33	□ 17:1-5	□ 17:6-13	□ 17:14-24	□ 17:25—18:11	□ 18:12-27
37	□ 18:28-40	□ 19:1-16	□ 19:17-30	□ 19:31-42	□ 20:1-13	□ 20:14-18	□ 20:19-22
38	□ 20:23-31	□ 21:1-14	□ 21:15-22	□ 21:23-25	□ Acts 1:1-8	□ 1:9-14	□ 1:15-26
39	□ 2:1-13	□ 2:14-21	□ 2:22-36	□ 2:37-41	□ 2:42-47	□ 3:1-18	□ 3:19—4:22
40	□ 4:23-37	□ 5:1-16	□ 5:17-32	□ 5:33-42	□ 6:1—7:1	□ 7:2-29	□ 7:30-60
41	□ 8:1-13	□ 8:14-25	□ 8:26-40	□ 9:1-19	□ 9:20-43	□ 10:1-16	□ 10:17-33
42	□ 10:34-48	□ 11:1-18	□ 11:19-30	□ 12:1-25	□ 13:1-12	□ 13:13-43	□ 13:44—14:5
43	□ 14:6-28	□ 15:1-12	□ 15:13-34	□ 15:35—16:5	□ 16:6-18	□ 16:19-40	□ 17:1-18
44	□ 17:19-34	□ 18:1-17	□ 18:18-28	□ 19:1-20	□ 19:21-41	□ 20:1-12	□ 20:13-38
45	□ 21:1-14	□ 21:15-26	□ 21:27-40	□ 22:1-21	□ 22:22-29	□ 22:30—23:11	□ 23:12-15
46	□ 23:16-30	□ 23:31—24:21	□ 24:22—25:5	□ 25:6-27	□ 26:1-13	□ 26:14-32	□ 27:1-26
47	□ 27:27—28:10	□ 28:11-22	□ 28:23-31	□ Rom 1:1-2	□ 1:3-7	□ 1:8-17	□ 1:18-25
48	□ 1:26—2:10	□ 2:11-29	□ 3:1-20	□ 3:21-31	□ 4:1-12	□ 4:13-25	□ 5:1-11
49	□ 5:12-17	□ 5:18—6:5	□ 6:6-11	□ 6:12-23	□ 7:1-12	□ 7:13-25	□ 8:1-2
50	□ 8:3-6	□ 8:7-13	□ 8:14-25	□ 8:26-39	□ 9:1-18	□ 9:19—10:3	□ 10:4-15
51	□ 10:16—11:10	□ 11:11-22	□ 11:23-36	□ 12:1-3	□ 12:4-21	□ 13:1-14	□ 14:1-12
52	□ 14:13-23	□ 15:1-13	□ 15:14-33	□ 16:1-5	□ 16:6-24	□ 16:25-27	□ 1 Cor 1:1-4

Reading Schedule for the Recovery Version of the New Testament with Footnotes

Wk.	Lord's Day	Monday	Tuesday	Wednesday	Thursday	Friday	Saturday
53	☐ 1 Cor 1:5-9	☐ 1:10-17	☐ 1:18-31	☐ 2:1-5	☐ 2:6-10	☐ 2:11-16	☐ 3:1-9
54	☐ 3:10-13	☐ 3:14-23	☐ 4:1-9	☐ 4:10-21	☐ 5:1-13	☐ 6:1-11	☐ 6:12-20
55	☐ 7:1-16	☐ 7:17-24	☐ 7:25-40	☐ 8:1-13	☐ 9:1-15	☐ 9:16-27	☐ 10:1-4
56	☐ 10:5-13	☐ 10:14-33	☐ 11:1-6	☐ 11:7-16	☐ 11:17-26	☐ 11:27-34	☐ 12:1-11
57	☐ 12:12-22	☐ 12:23-31	☐ 13:1-13	☐ 14:1-12	☐ 14:13-25	☐ 14:26-33	☐ 14:34-40
58	☐ 15:1-19	☐ 15:20-28	☐ 15:29-34	☐ 15:35-49	☐ 15:50-58	☐ 16:1-9	☐ 16:10-24
59	☐ 2 Cor 1:1-4	☐ 1:5-14	☐ 1:15-22	☐ 1:23—2:11	☐ 2:12-17	☐ 3:1-6	☐ 3:7-11
60	☐ 3:12-18	☐ 4:1-6	☐ 4:7-12	☐ 4:13-18	☐ 5:1-8	☐ 5:9-15	☐ 5:16-21
61	☐ 6:1-13	☐ 6:14—7:4	☐ 7:5-16	☐ 8:1-15	☐ 8:16-24	☐ 9:1-15	☐ 10:1-6
62	☐ 10:7-18	☐ 11:1-15	☐ 11:16-33	☐ 12:1-10	☐ 12:11-21	☐ 13:1-10	☐ 13:11-14
63	☐ Gal 1:1-5	☐ 1:6-14	☐ 1:15-24	☐ 2:1-13	☐ 2:14-21	☐ 3:1-4	☐ 3:5-14
64	☐ 3:15-22	☐ 3:23-29	☐ 4:1-7	☐ 4:8-20	☐ 4:21-31	☐ 5:1-12	☐ 5:13-21
65	☐ 5:22-26	☐ 6:1-10	☐ 6:11-15	☐ 6:16-18	☐ Eph 1:1-3	☐ 1:4-6	☐ 1:7-10
66	☐ 1:11-14	☐ 1:15-18	☐ 1:19-23	☐ 2:1-5	☐ 2:6-10	☐ 2:11-14	☐ 2:15-18
67	☐ 2:19-22	☐ 3:1-7	☐ 3:8-13	☐ 3:14-18	☐ 3:19-21	☐ 4:1-4	☐ 4:5-10
68	☐ 4:11-16	☐ 4:17-24	☐ 4:25-32	☐ 5:1-10	☐ 5:11-21	☐ 5:22-26	☐ 5:27-33
69	☐ 6:1-9	☐ 6:10-14	☐ 6:15-18	☐ 6:19-24	☐ Phil 1:1-7	☐ 1:8-18	☐ 1:19-26
70	☐ 1:27—2:4	☐ 2:5-11	☐ 2:12-16	☐ 2:17-30	☐ 3:1-6	☐ 3:7-11	☐ 3:12-16
71	☐ 3:17-21	☐ 4:1-9	☐ 4:10-23	☐ Col 1:1-8	☐ 1:9-13	☐ 1:14-23	☐ 1:24-29
72	☐ 2:1-7	☐ 2:8-15	☐ 2:16-23	☐ 3:1-4	☐ 3:5-15	☐ 3:16-25	☐ 4:1-18
73	☐ 1 Thes 1:1-3	☐ 1:4-10	☐ 2:1-12	☐ 2:13—3:5	☐ 3:6-13	☐ 4:1-10	☐ 4:11—5:11
74	☐ 5:12-28	☐ 2 Thes 1:1-12	☐ 2:1-17	☐ 3:1-18	☐ 1 Tim 1:1-2	☐ 1:3-4	☐ 1:5-14
75	☐ 1:15-20	☐ 2:1-7	☐ 2:8-15	☐ 3:1-13	☐ 3:14—4:5	☐ 4:6-16	☐ 5:1-25
76	☐ 6:1-10	☐ 6:11-21	☐ 2 Tim 1:1-10	☐ 1:11-18	☐ 2:1-15	☐ 2:16-26	☐ 3:1-13
77	☐ 3:14—4:8	☐ 4:9-22	☐ Titus 1:1-4	☐ 1:5-16	☐ 2:1-15	☐ 3:1-8	☐ 3:9-15
78	☐ Philem 1:1-11	☐ 1:12-25	☐ Heb 1:1-2	☐ 1:3-5	☐ 1:6-14	☐ 2:1-9	☐ 2:10-18

Reading Schedule for the Recovery Version of the New Testament with Footnotes

Wk.	Lord's Day	Monday	Tuesday	Wednesday	Thursday	Friday	Saturday
79	Heb 3:1-6	3:7-19	4:1-9	4:10-13	4:14-16	5:1-10	5:11—6:3
80	6:4-8	6:9-20	7:1-10	7:11-28	8:1-6	8:7-13	9:1-4
81	9:5-14	9:15-28	10:1-18	10:19-28	10:29-39	11:1-6	11:7-19
82	11:20-31	11:32-40	12:1-2	12:3-13	12:14-17	12:18-26	12:27-29
83	13:1-7	13:8-12	13:13-15	13:16-25	James 1:1-8	1:9-18	1:19-27
84	2:1-13	2:14-26	3:1-18	4:1-10	4:11-17	5:1-12	5:13-20
85	1 Pet 1:1-2	1:3-4	1:5	1:6-9	1:10-12	1:13-17	1:18-25
86	2:1-3	2:4-8	2:9-17	2:18-25	3:1-13	3:14-22	4:1-6
87	4:7-16	4:17-19	5:1-4	5:5-9	5:10-14	2 Pet 1:1-2	1:3-4
88	1:5-8	1:9-11	1:12-18	1:19-21	2:1-3	2:4-11	2:12-22
89	3:1-6	3:7-9	3:10-12	3:13-15	3:16	3:17-18	1 John 1:1-2
90	1:3-4	1:5	1:6	1:7	1:8-10	2:1-2	2:3-11
91	2:12-14	2:15-19	2:20-23	2:24-27	2:28-29	3:1-5	3:6-10
92	3:11-18	3:19-24	4:1-6	4:7-11	4:12-15	4:16—5:3	5:4-13
93	5:14-17	5:18-21	2 John 1:1-3	1:4-9	1:10-13	3 John 1:1-6	1:7-14
94	Jude 1:1-4	1:5-10	1:11-19	1:20-25	Rev 1:1-3	1:4-6	1:7-11
95	1:12-13	1:14-16	1:17-20	2:1-6	2:7	2:8-9	2:10-11
96	2:12-14	2:15-17	2:18-23	2:24-29	3:1-3	3:4-6	3:7-9
97	3:10-13	3:14-18	3:19-22	4:1-5	4:6-7	4:8-11	5:1-6
98	5:7-14	6:1-8	6:9-17	7:1-8	7:9-17	8:1-6	8:7-12
99	8:13—9:11	9:12-21	10:1-4	10:5-11	11:1-4	11:5-14	11:15-19
100	12:1-4	12:5-9	12:10-18	13:1-10	13:11-18	14:1-5	14:6-12
101	14:13-20	15:1-8	16:1-12	16:13-21	17:1-6	17:7-18	18:1-8
102	18:9—19:4	19:5-10	19:11-16	19:17-21	20:1-6	20:7-10	20:11-15
103	21:1	21:2	21:3-8	21:9-13	21:14-18	21:19-21	21:22-27
104	22:1	22:2	22:3-11	22:12-15	22:16-17	22:18-21	

Week 1 — Day 4   Today's verses

Rom. 5:17   For if, by the offense of the one, death reigned through the one, much more those who receive the abundance of grace and of the gift of righteousness will reign in life through the One, Jesus Christ.

Week 1 — Day 5   Today's verses

2 Cor. 5:18-20   But all things are out from God, who has reconciled us to Himself through Christ and has given to us the ministry of reconciliation; namely, that God in Christ was reconciling the world to Himself, not accounting their offenses to them, and has put in us the word of reconciliation. On behalf of Christ then we are ambassadors, as God entreats *you* through us; we beseech *you* on behalf of Christ, Be reconciled to God.

Week 1 — Day 6   Today's verses

2 Cor. 4:1   Therefore having this ministry as we have been shown mercy, we do not lose heart.

2 Cor. 11:2-3   For I am jealous over you with a jealousy of God; for I betrothed you to one husband to present *you* as a pure virgin to Christ. But I fear lest somehow, as the serpent deceived Eve by his craftiness, your thoughts would be corrupted from the simplicity and the purity toward Christ.

Date _____

Week 1 — Day 1   Today's verses

Rev. 21:2   And I saw the holy city, New Jerusalem, coming down out of heaven from God, prepared as a bride adorned for her husband.

22:1-2   And he showed me a river of water of life, bright as crystal, proceeding out of the throne of God and of the Lamb in the middle of its street. And on this side and on that side of the river was the tree of life, producing twelve fruits, yielding its fruit each month; and the leaves of the tree are for the healing of the nations.

Date _____

Week 1 — Day 2   Today's verses

2 Pet. 1:4   Through which He has granted to us precious and exceedingly great promises that through these you might become partakers of the divine nature, having escaped the corruption which is in the world by lust.

Date _____

Week 1 — Day 3   Today's verses

2 Cor. 3:3   Since you are being manifested that you are a letter of Christ ministered by us, inscribed not with ink but with the Spirit of the living God; not in tablets of stone but in tablets of hearts of flesh.

6   Who has also made us sufficient as ministers of a new covenant, *ministers* not of the letter but of the Spirit; for the letter kills, but the Spirit gives life.

9   For if there is glory with the ministry of condemnation, much more the ministry of righteousness abounds with glory.

Date _____

Week 2 — Day 4

Today's verses

Gal. 2:20 I am crucified with Christ; and it is no longer I who live, but it is Christ who lives in me; and the life which I now live in the flesh I live in faith, the *faith* of the Son of God, who loved me and gave Himself up for me.

Phil. 3:10-11 To know Him and the power of His resurrection and the fellowship of His sufferings, being conformed to His death, if perhaps I may attain to the out-resurrection from the dead.

Date _____

Week 2 — Day 5

Today's verses

1 Cor. 12:12-13 For even as the body is one and has many members, yet all the members of the body, being many, are one body, so also is the Christ. For also in one Spirit we were all baptized into one Body, whether Jews or Greeks, whether slaves or free, and were all given to drink one Spirit.

26-27 And whether one member suffers, all the members suffer with *it*; or one member is glorified, all the members rejoice with *it*. Now you are the Body of Christ, and members individually.

Date _____

Week 2 — Day 6

Today's verses

Eph. 3:16-17 That He would grant you, according to the riches of His glory, to be strengthened with power through His Spirit into the inner man, that Christ may make His home in your hearts through faith....

Col. 3:15 And let the peace of Christ arbitrate in your hearts, to which also you were called in one Body; and be thankful.

Rev. 19:7 Let us rejoice and exult, and let us give the glory to Him, for the marriage of the Lamb has come, and His wife has made herself ready.

Date _____

Week 2 — Day 1

Today's verses

John 1:12-13 But as many as received Him, to them He gave the authority to become children of God, to those who believe into His name, who were begotten not of blood, nor of the will of the flesh, nor of the will of man, but of God.

1 John 3:2 Beloved, now we are children of God, and it has not yet been manifested what we will be. We know that if He is manifested, we will be like Him because we will see Him even as He is.

Date _____

Week 2 — Day 2

Today's verses

Rom. 1:3-4 ...His Son, who came out of the seed of David according to the flesh, who was designated the Son of God in power according to the Spirit of holiness out of the resurrection of the dead, Jesus Christ our Lord.

John 14:20 In that day you will know that I am in My Father, and you in Me, and I in you.

Date _____

Week 2 — Day 3

Today's verses

John 20:22 And when He had said this, He breathed into *them* and said to them, Receive the Holy Spirit.

2 Cor. 3:17-18 And the Lord is the Spirit; and where the Spirit of the Lord is, there is freedom. But we all with unveiled face, beholding and reflecting like a mirror the glory of the Lord, are being transformed into the same image from glory to glory, even as from the Lord Spirit.

Date _____

Week 3 — Day 4 Today's verses

Eph. ...The Head, Christ, out from whom all
4:15-16 the Body, being joined together and
being knit together through every joint of
the rich supply and *through* the opera-
tion in the measure of each one part,
causes the growth of the Body unto the
building up of itself in love.

5:21 Being subject to one another in the fear of
Christ.

Date

Week 3 — Day 5 Today's verses

John Do you not believe that I am in the Father
14:10-11 and the Father is in Me? The words that I
say to you I do not speak from Myself, but
the Father who abides in Me does His
works. Believe Me that I am in the Father
and the Father is in Me; but if not, believe
because of the works themselves.

2 Cor. The grace of the Lord Jesus Christ and the
13:14 love of God and the fellowship of the
Holy Spirit be with you all.

Date

Week 3 — Day 6 Today's verses

John That they all may be one; even as You,
17:21 Father, are in Me and I in You, that they
also may be in Us; that the world may
believe that You have sent Me.

Eph. [That you] may be full of strength to
3:18-19 apprehend with all the saints what the
breadth and length and height and depth
are and to know the knowledge-surpassing love of Christ, that you may be filled
unto all the fullness of God.

Date

Week 3 — Day 1 Today's verses

Acts Therefore let all the house of Israel know
2:36 assuredly that God has made Him both
Lord and Christ, this Jesus whom you
have crucified.

Phil. ...God highly exalted Him and bestowed
2:9-11 on Him the name which is above every
name, that in the name of Jesus every
knee should bow, of those who are in
heaven and on earth and under the earth,
and every tongue should openly confess
that Jesus Christ is Lord to the glory of
God the Father.

Date

Week 3 — Day 2 Today's verses

Matt. And Jesus came and spoke to them,
28:18 saying, All authority has been given to
Me in heaven and on earth.

Eph. But holding to truth in love, we may grow
4:15 up into Him in all things, who is the
Head, Christ.

Col. And He is the Head of the Body, the
1:18 church; He is the beginning, the Firstborn
from the dead, that He Himself might
have the first place in all things.

Date

Week 3 — Day 3 Today's verses

Eph. And He subjected all things under His
1:22-23 feet and gave Him *to be* Head over all
things to the church, which is His Body,
the fullness of the One who fills all in all.

Col. ...Holding the Head, out from whom all
2:19 the Body, being richly supplied and knit
together by means of the joints and
sinews, grows with the growth of God.

Date

| Week 4 — Day 4 | Today's verses | Week 4 — Day 5 | Today's verses | Week 4 — Day 6 | Today's verses |

Week 4 — Day 4 — Today's verses

Rev. 5:6 And I saw...a Lamb standing as having *just* been slain, having seven horns and seven eyes, which are the seven Spirits of God sent forth into all the earth.

2:1 To the messenger of the church in Ephesus write: These things says He who holds the seven stars in His right hand, He who walks in the midst of the seven golden lampstands.

2:7 He who has an ear, let him hear what the Spirit says to the churches. To him who overcomes, to him I will give to eat of the tree of life, which is in the Paradise of God.

Date

Week 4 — Day 5 — Today's verses

Rev. 12:5 And she brought forth a son, a man-child, who is to shepherd all the nations with an iron rod; and her child was caught up to God and to His throne.

14:4 ...These were purchased from among men *as* firstfruits to God and to the Lamb.

Date

Week 4 — Day 6 — Today's verses

Exo. 23:19 The first of the firstfruits of your ground you shall bring into the house of Jehovah your God.

Rev. 14:4-5 These are they who have not been defiled with women, for they are virgins. These are they who follow the Lamb wherever He may go. These were purchased from among men *as* firstfruits to God and to the Lamb. And in their mouth no lie was found; they are without blemish.

22:17 And the Spirit and the bride say, Come!...

Date

Week 4 — Day 1 — Today's verses

John 1:1, 14 ...The Word was God....And the Word became flesh and tabernacled among us....

20:22 And when He had said this, He breathed into *them* and said to them, Receive the Holy Spirit.

Rev. 1:4-5 ...Grace to you and peace from Him who is and who was and who is coming, and from the seven Spirits who are before His throne, and from Jesus Christ...

Date

Week 4 — Day 2 — Today's verses

Rev. 4:5 ...And *there were* seven lamps of fire burning before the throne, which are the seven Spirits of God.

5:6 And I saw in the midst of the throne...a Lamb standing as having *just* been slain, having seven horns and seven eyes, which are the seven Spirits of God sent forth into all the earth.

Date

Week 4 — Day 3 — Today's verses

Rev. 2:1-2, 4 To the messenger of the church in Ephesus write:...I know your works and your labor and your endurance....But I have *one thing* against you, that you have left your first love.

3:1 And to the messenger of the church in Sardis write: These things says He who has the seven Spirits of God and the seven stars: I know your works, that you have a name that you are living, and yet you are dead.

Date

Rev. 12:3-4 And another sign was seen in heaven; and behold, *there was* a great red dragon, having seven heads and ten horns....And the dragon stood before the woman who was about to bring forth, so that when she brings forth he might devour her child.

11 And they overcame him because of the blood of the Lamb and because of the word of their testimony, and they loved not their soul-life even unto death.

Date

Week 5 — Day 1   Today's verses

Gen. 3:15 And I will put enmity between you and the woman and between your seed and her seed; he will bruise you on the head, but you will bruise him on the heel.

Rev. 12:9-10 And the great dragon was cast down, the ancient serpent, he who is called the Devil and Satan, he who deceives the whole inhabited earth; he was cast to the earth....And I heard a loud voice in heaven saying, Now has come the salvation and the power and the kingdom of our God and the authority of His Christ, for the accuser of our brothers has been cast down, who accuses them before our God day and night.

Date

Rev. 12:5 And she brought forth a son, a man-child, who is to shepherd all the nations with an iron rod; and her child was caught up to God and to His throne.

Eph. 6:10-11 Finally, be empowered in the Lord and in the might of His strength. Put on the whole armor of God that you may be able to stand against the stratagems of the devil.

2 Tim. 1:9 Who has saved us and called us with a holy calling, not according to our works but according to His own purpose...

Date

Week 5 — Day 2   Today's verses

Rev. 12:1-2 A great sign was seen in heaven: a woman clothed with the sun, and the moon underneath her feet, and on her head a crown of twelve stars; and she was with child, and she cried out, travailing in birth and being in pain to bring forth.

Gal. 4:19 My children, with whom I travail again in birth until Christ is formed in you.

Date

Matt. 6:9-10 You then pray in this way: Our Father who is in the heavens, Your name be sanctified; Your kingdom come; Your will be done, as in heaven, *so* also on earth.

Rev. 11:15 ...There were loud voices in heaven, saying, The kingdom of the world has become the *kingdom* of our Lord and of His Christ, and He will reign forever and ever.

Week 5 — Day 3   Today's verses

2 Cor. 11:2 For I am jealous over you with a jealousy of God; for I betrothed you to one husband to present *you* as a pure virgin to Christ.

Eph. 5:24 But as the church is subject to Christ, so also *let* the wives *be subject* to their husbands in everything.

Phil. 1:21 For to me, to live is Christ...

Date

Week 6 — Day 4

Today's verses

Lev. 1:1   Then Jehovah called to Moses and spoke to him out of the Tent of Meeting....

Psa. 133:1, 3   Behold, how good and how pleasant it is for brothers to dwell in unity!...For there Jehovah commanded the blessing: Life forever.

Date

Week 6 — Day 1

Today's verses

Col. 1:17-18   And He is before all things, and all things cohere in Him; and He is the Head of the Body, the church; He is the beginning, the Firstborn from the dead, that He Himself might have the first place in all things.

Date

Week 6 — Day 5

Today's verses

John 17:11   ...Holy Father, keep them in Your name, which You have given to Me, that they may be one even as We are.

17   Sanctify them in the truth; Your word is truth.

22   And the glory which You have given Me I have given to them, that they may be one, even as We are one.

Date

Week 6 — Day 2

Today's verses

1 Tim. 1:3-4   Even as I exhorted you, when I was going into Macedonia, to remain in Ephesus in order that you might charge certain ones not to teach different things nor to give heed to myths and unending genealogies, which produce questionings rather than God's economy, which is in faith.

Rom. 15:6   That with one accord you may with one mouth glorify the God and Father of our Lord Jesus Christ.

Date

Week 6 — Day 6

Today's verses

Deut. 12:5   But to the place which Jehovah your God will choose out of all your tribes to put His name, to His habitation, shall you seek, and there shall you go.

Num. 32:5   And they said, If we have found favor in your sight, let this land be given to your servants for a possession; do not make us cross over the Jordan.

Date

Week 6 — Day 3

Today's verses

1 Cor. 1:10   Now I beseech you, brothers, through the name of our Lord Jesus Christ, that you all speak the same thing and *that* there be no divisions among you, but *that* you be attuned in the same mind and in the same opinion.

Rom. 15:6   That with one accord you may with one mouth glorify the God and Father of our Lord Jesus Christ.

Date